RUNNING TRAINING LIKE A BUSINESS

RUNNING TRAINING LIKE A BUSINESS

Delivering Unmistakable Value

David van Adelsberg
& Edward A. Trolley

THE FORUM CORPORATION

 Berrett-Koehler Publishers, Inc.
San Francisco

Berrett-Koehler Publishers, Inc.
450 Sansome Street, Suite 1200
San Francisco, CA 94111-3320
Tel: (415) 288-0260   Fax: (415) 362-2512   www.bkconnection.com

Ordering Information

Quantity sales. Special discounts are available on quantity purchases by corporations, associations, and others. For details, contact the "Special Sales Department" at the Berrett-Koehler address above.

Individual sales. Berrett-Koehler publications are available through most bookstores. They can also be ordered direct from Berrett-Koehler:
Tel: (800) 929-2929; Fax: (802) 864-7626; www.bkconnection.com

Orders for college textbook/course adoption use. Please contact Berrett-Koehler:
Tel: (800) 929-2929; Fax: (802) 864-7626.

Orders by U.S. trade bookstores and wholesalers. Please contact Publishers Group West, 1700 Fourth Street, Berkeley, CA 94710. Tel: (510) 528-1444; Fax (510) 528-3444.

Printed in the United States of America

 Printed on acid-free and recycled paper that is composed of 85% recovered fiber, including 15% post consumer waste.

Library of Congress Cataloging-in-Publication Data
  Van Adelsberg, David, 1960–
    Running training like a business : delivering unmistakable value /
  David van Adelsberg & Edward Trolley. – 1st ed.
      p. cm.
    Includes bibliographical references (p.) and index.
    ISBN 1-57675-059-0
    1. Employees, Training of. 2. Training. I. Trolley, Edward A., 1948–   .
  II. Title.
    HF5549.5.T7V22 1999   99-28829
    658.3' 124–dc21
                                                                 CIP

First Edition
05 04 03 02 01 00 99   10 9 8 7 6 5 4 3 2 1

Editing: Vivian Jaquette   Art: Mendocino Graphics
Proofreading: Suzanne Byerley   Interior Design: Elizabeth Petersen
Indexing: Paula C. Durbin-Westby   Production: Linda Jupiter, Jupiter Productions

To my parents and grandparents, who survived years of extreme hardship with dignity, strength, and optimism. And to Lisa and Hunter, whose patience and love have taught me to see the possibilities of each day.

—David

To Becky and Emily, for their continued love, patience, and support, and to my parents, who would have been proud.

— Ed

Contents

Preface

Let's talk about your investments—specifically, your investments in training.

Businesses invest vast sums of money and significant portions of their productive capacity in training and development (T&D). It's common for top corporations to provide from 30 to well over 100 hours of training to each employee every year. Smaller businesses frequently invest even more heavily in training as a percentage of payroll. Reliable sources estimate that, overall, annual U.S. corporate investments in T&D exceed $56 *billion*.[1]

Impressive as that figure is, we believe it is really just the tip of the iceberg. (We'll tell you about the hidden costs of training in Chapter 3.) When executives first glimpse the *true* cost of training, beyond the mere fraction represented in most T&D budgets, they're often staggered by the facts.

Training professionals invest something every bit as precious—their *careers*. We see training people pour themselves into their work day after day. Training is their craft. And for the best of them, it's more than a career; it's a passion. Nothing else can explain why so many trainers give so much to their jobs.

So, whether you're a customer of training or a provider of training, you have a lot at stake. All that time, money, and energy could easily be dedicated to other practical purposes.

Are you satisfied with the return on your investment in training? If you answered No, you're not alone.

Business leaders who buy training recognize that, in a knowledge economy, learning is central to business success. Corporations worldwide have ramped up their investments in T&D. And technological advances continue to fuel executives' excitement about what training might do for them.

But there's a problem. Many business leaders say that T&D remains "out of the loop" strategically, that it too often operates like "something separate from the business," and that they don't see enough tangible returns on their T&D investments. When training is perceived this way, neither the customers who pay the bills nor the professionals who dedicate themselves to the work can feel fully satisfied.

Our solution? Transform training from running as a *function* to running like a *business*. That is the key, we've found, to delivering the kind of value that results-minded executives recognize, appreciate, respect, and increasingly demand.

What does Running Training Like a Business mean? The core of the concept is to make everything training does simultaneously more effective and efficient. Being *effective* means delivering training services that tangibly help businesses to achieve their goals. Being *efficient* means making the true costs of training clearly evident and highly acceptable to its customers.

To become more effective and efficient, training adopts the values of its customers and eliminates the ambiguities that have traditionally clouded its mission. Training's mission becomes unashamedly *economic*. Education is still what training does. But business education is a means to business results, not an end in itself.

Training organizations that run like a business aren't allocated a corporate budget. They in effect sell their services every day, as does any business enterprise. The survival of this training enterprise therefore rests on its ability to address strongly felt customer needs.

For most training organizations, Running Training Like a Business will begin with a transformation. This book explains what is entailed in turning a traditional training function into a training enterprise that pursues missions clearly vital to its customers' business strategies, and offers the range of resources required to fulfill those missions efficiently, consistently, and profitably.

The benefits of Running Training Like a Business are immense. Best of all, this tide raises all ships.

Business leaders get to work with training organizations that are thoroughly attuned to business issues and utterly dedicated to developing the skills, aptitudes, and attitudes executives deem vital for improved business results. Running Training Like a Business also reduces or even eliminates fixed costs for T&D and yields much more efficient forms of training activity. That frees substantial corporate resources for business leaders to invest in enhancing the core competencies of their companies.

Training professionals gain a clearer understanding of how their business customers think, what drives their behavior, and what they truly value. In fact, Running Training Like a Business propels internal as well as external T&D providers into the mainstream of their customers' business strategies, makes their services a more integral and valued resource for fulfilling those strategies, and increases T&D's stature in the business world.

The people who participate in training benefit as well. A training enterprise delivers services that line managers elect to buy. Participants in training will know, then, that their boss *wants* them to be there. Further, they'll be learning skills that business leaders clearly value. That's bound to help them get ahead in a marketplace where employees with practical, vital skills are in demand.

The concept of Running Training Like a Business evolved from our work with a wide range of organizations over the past six years. Some (but not all) of those organizations are cited in this book. Our experiences with Moore Corporation, Mellon Bank, Texas Instruments Materials & Controls, NCR, NatWest UK, and Oracle offer excellent insights into why some organizations choose to pursue this transformation. They also serve as practical examples of what one must do in the first several phases of the transformation.

We've often worked with customers through a construct we call an Insourcing Alliance, by which a business brings an outside training resource *inside* its company, merging the best of its existing T&D staff with those of the external training organization to form a training enterprise. This new organization—the Insourcing Alliance—replaces the former T&D function. Because most of our experience is based on this construct, we'll refer often in these pages to these alliances, which are now operating or taking shape in a handful of pioneering businesses.

We will also stress, however, that the Insourcing Alliance is but one of several options for pursuing the transformation to Running Training Like a Business. We'll describe, for example, an approach Kaiser Permanente of California calls an Alliance Network, as well as successful transformations implemented almost entirely from within at Motorola and General Electric.

In sum, we don't have all the answers. Nor can we offer absolute best practices for Running Training Like a Business. Those practices are still being shaped. What we can do is describe an emerging concept, one which we're still learning about ourselves, but which has already demonstrated remarkable power to make training significantly more valuable to everyone in business. We can also share experiences and insights from organizations that have embraced these principles and are turning them into reality. Finally, we can help your organization start down this path, too, if that is what you choose to do.

Toward those ends, we've divided this book into three sections. Chapters 1 through 3 make the business case for transforming traditional training organizations into training enterprises. We wrote these chapters for every executive who buys training services, and for all the professionals who provide them.

Chapters 4 through 8 are more prescriptive. They explore, in some detail, the major phases of transforming a traditional training function into training that runs like a business. They also delineate the key steps to successfully completing each phase.

Chapters 9 and 10 describe the fully formed training enterprise. They offer a glimpse into how Running Training Like a Business yields satisfying returns to all the investors in training—training providers, training participants and, most important, training's customers.

Acknowledgments

The road from resolving to write a book to seeing that book in print held more twists and turns than we expected. Fortunately, many fine people were there to help us along the way.

Our families and friends supported us from start to finish. Their ongoing encouragement was uplifting as well as sustaining. Special thanks to The Langmuirs for inviting us to use their lovely place on Martha's Vineyard.

Steven Piersanti and the rest of the Berrett-Koehler team worked tirelessly to help this pair of first-time authors shape and focus their ideas into a book that would best serve readers. Tom Varian joined those efforts at a crucial juncture. His writing skills and experience in developing books proved indispensable to the task.

Our firm, The Forum Corporation, placed its faith in our mission. It also kept fuel in our tanks. Thank you, John Humphrey and John Harris, for your counsel and steadfast support.

Others who played a major role in shaping this book include Diane Hessan, Robert Wood, Annie Post, Anne Palmer, Jennifer Potter-Brotman, Mary Maloney, Allen Roberts, Mahbod Seraji, Ed Boswell, and Ellen Foley.

Judy Panichi, Bronwen Barnett, Kim Smith, Gene Cox, Chris Allen, Susan Quinn, Anne Lockhart, Debbie Ansary, Richard Harris, David and Erik Leifer, and Dave Alhadeff also made timely and important contributions.

In addition, we'd like to thank Forum's Danielle Busack, Susan Marsh, Kathleen Gilroy, Gregg Johnson, Sarene Byrne, David Blount, Jane Carroll, Richard Whiteley, Harland Hunter, Melissa Thomas, Dick Comer, J. Miguez, Robin Martin, and Joe Wheeler for their advice and efforts.

Our sincere appreciation goes out, as well, to the half-dozen individuals recruited by Berrett-Koehler to comment on our draft manuscript. Their insights and suggestions were well-considered, constructive, and thoroughly helpful.

Last, and perhaps most important, we would like to acknowledge the essential contributions of these customers and partners, many of whom are cited in these pages:

Ty Alexander

Chris Bottomley

George Brennan

Ken Broker

Susan Christie

Bill Cullom

Paul Earley

Madeline Fassler

Elizabeth Knobloch

David McAndrews

Dennis McGurer

Nigel Pettinger

Irene Shadoan

Michael Spurling

Jackie Stephens

Ian Tomlinson-Roe

Rolf Woldt

Special Recognition

The concepts at the heart of this book originated at DuPont. Six years ago, a handful of DuPont managers hit upon some intriguing ideas about how to make training and development significantly more effective and efficient. In keeping with its history of innovation, DuPont then offered itself as a proving ground where those promising notions could be tested, developed, and refined. Words strain to express our gratitude to DuPont for taking that chance, and for inviting The Forum Corporation to be its collaborator in the endeavor.

The story of the experimental Learning Alliance DuPont fashioned with Forum has since been recounted many times in many different publications. To avoid repeating an oft-told tale, these pages focus on the subsequent development of the approach we call Running Training Like a Business.

Let the record show, however, that DuPont is where the approach sprang to life. DuPont's leaders chartered a new training organization dedicated to the belief that T&D could and should be more firmly linked to business needs. They then made this new training organization DuPont's global provider of T&D. In turn, people throughout that great corporation tempered the new concepts with their wisdom, and DuPont's groundbreaking Learning Alliance still thrives today.

So, to all our friends and customers at DuPont, we offer this hearty acknowledgment. You changed T&D—forever and for the better.

PART I

The Business Case
for
Transformation

In Chapter 1 we'll ponder the opportunities as well as the risks that now confront training, in light of T&D's often paradoxical relationship with results-driven executives.

In Chapter 2 we'll consider how T&D may unintentionally distance itself from the business mainstream, thereby limiting its capacity to produce more tangible returns on customers' investments in training.

In Chapter 3 we'll explain how Running Training Like a Business enables T&D to deliver more of the unmistakable value its business customers demand.

1
Sold on Learning

"It was the best of times, it was the worst of times." Say, that's not a bad way to start a book! Too bad Dickens beat us to it. The celebrated opening line from *A Tale of Two Cities* aptly describes the bittersweet world of training today.

This certainly *could* be the best of times for T&D. Executives see a widening gap between the skills and knowledge that businesses require versus those that the workforce can offer. "The need for skilled employees has never been keener," declared a recent article in *Fortune*. "One-in-ten information technology jobs sits unfilled, and companies are almost as hungry for workers adept at so-called soft skills."[1]

As a result, there is now virtual consensus among executives that learning must be a major factor in their ongoing strategies for business success. Even Wall Street, never a noted fan of T&D, has caught scent of this trend. "A tsunami of cash is poised over the [training] industry," trumpets an article in *Training & Development* magazine. "Within two years, it will have reshaped everything."[2] *Training Magazine* reports, "The prevailing thesis on Wall Street is that knowledge workers will require more education and more training than ever before. As a result, corporate training budgets will increase substantially, which will mean more money flowing into the coffers of companies that sell training."[3]

Investors who sense a link between growing demand for knowledge workers and increased demand for corporate education are definitely on to something. Research reported in the *Journal of Applied Psychology* showed that the productivity differential between top performers and low performers in a given job grows exponentially as job complexity increases (Figure 1-1).

The best worker flipping burgers in a McDonald's, for example, might be as little as three times more productive than the worst, whereas the best performers doing skilled work on an auto assembly line (a job of medium complexity) might be 12 times more produc-

Figure 1-1: Productivity Range by Job Complexity

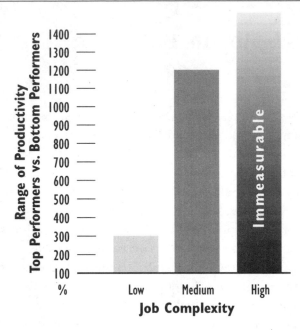

tive than certain others doing the same job. At the high end of the complexity scale, where knowledge workers such as investment bankers and engineers operate, the productivity differences between top performers and bottom performers reportedly grow so vast, they are virtually immeasurable.[4]

This means that in a knowledge-based economy, improving worker performance could yield unprecedented improvement in the overall productivity, competitiveness, and long-term performance of a business. That's why so many of today's business leaders are sold on learning.

Jack Welch is a prime example. "In the end," says the Chief Executive Officer of General Electric, "the desire and ability of an organization to continuously learn from any source anywhere and rapidly convert this learning into action, is its ultimate competitive advantage."[5] More than a few executives now share this point of view—a circumstance that should make this "the best of times" for T&D.

Ends and Means

With such powerful trends combining to thrust learning into the spotlight, what could instead make these "the worst of times" for training?

Executives are keenly aware that training is but a means to learning. And while most business leaders are now sold on the idea that *learning* is crucial, some harbor serious doubts about whether the *training* in which they invest consistently yields learning that truly helps the business.

An attitude survey conducted in 1997 by U.K.-based Oxford Training, for example, asked line managers and their T&D counterparts in 65 major companies to react to 76 statements covering Training and Development services. A key finding of the study was summarized this way: "Line managers are significantly more reticent about the actual strategic impact of training than are training managers and professionals."[6]

We've encountered plenty of anecdotal evidence to corroborate that finding. "Our CEO says, 'When it's all said and done, the one competitive advantage is the employee.' And I can tell you, when he says that learning is vital, he means it," says Denny McGurer, Vice President for T&D at Moore Corporation. "But for a lot of years, T&D had just about no credibility here. Management resented paying for it. They didn't question the relevance of learning. They questioned the relevance of *T&D*."

That distinction seems to be lost on some in T&D. Why else would the profession spend so much time touting the business value of learning, when it is the business value of *training* that executives have been known to question? Indeed, executives' growing appetite for learning—combined with their doubts about the business value of training—is leading more than a few business leaders to look hard at their T&D investments.

"Fixed" training costs—those that are embedded in the business—are likely to come under especially intense executive scrutiny because, these days, fixed costs might as well walk around wearing a "kick me" sign. Salaries and permanent training facilities are two examples of "fixed" T&D costs. They can't be quickly dialed up and

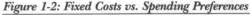

Figure 1-2: Fixed Costs vs. Spending Preferences

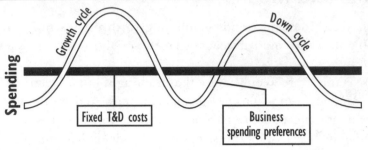

down by executives to fuel growth in times of opportunity or to protect profits when sales dip, as can the cost of vendors and other "variable" costs.

Executives are under relentless pressure to show strong earnings. So even when a business falters just slightly, fixed costs can look like a knife poised inches from the CEO's heart. Many executives will then look to slash budgets for any and all items not directly linked to short-term revenue and profit generation. When they come to the line item for T&D, they may simply chop 20 percent or more off the top. That is often not a great decision, mind you, but what choice do they really have? No one has offered them data or analysis to demonstrate the business value training delivers. And there's that earnings number to hit at the end of the quarter. . . .

Recessions have always been among "the worst of times" for training. But as the emerging knowledge economy raises expectations of T&D, executives' patience with training of uncertain business value may be just as strained during periods of business growth. T&D should not expect to receive the benefit of the doubt. Rather, it should assume that executives will demand more unmistakable value in return for their training investments.

Comparisons to Information Technology

The recent past of Information Technology (IT) may offer some sound lessons for making the future "the best of times" for T&D. Consider these similarities between where IT was a decade or two ago and where T&D is today:

- Both are traditionally "backwater" functions thrust suddenly by the changing demands of business toward the top of executives' strategic agendas.

- Neither function is very well understood by executives.

- Both are "big budget" items, made up largely of fixed costs.

- The economic impact of both is difficult to measure.

- Both functions are staffed (and often led) by people perceived to have plenty of "technical know-how" but a questionable grasp of business in general.

- Both operate as distinct subcultures within the larger business culture.

- Both are known to frustrate executives, who see practical business application lagging behind breakthroughs in available technology.

That last comparison may be the most significant. In the 1970s and 1980s, executives were excited about the *potential* of emerging computer and telecommunications technologies to serve their businesses. They were sold on the idea that IT, effectively applied, could drive business success. We can say with confidence, though, that many executives were impatient for IT to deliver clear efficiencies, new opportunities, and decisive competitive advantages to the business.

Successful IT organizations saw this. They didn't waste much time trying to sell business executives on the potential of technology. Rather, they focused on making information technology more relevant, accessible, and practical for business application. Today, businesses use computers for everything from prospecting for customers to designing new products to keeping their books. Information Technology has automated repetitive tasks, dramatically speeded business operations, linked businesses electronically to their customers, opened vast new electronic marketing and distribution channels (like the Internet), and created lucrative new categories of products.

Such tangible contributions earned IT a place at the table where important business decisions are made. Most sizable companies now have a Chief Information Officer among their top executives. In sum, IT professionals made this "the best of times" for their field. And they did it by turning their technology's potential into unmistakable value.

Top business leaders appear to be every bit as sold on learning today as they were sold on information technology two decades ago. And more than a few seem determined to make learning an equally explicit component of their business strategy. General Electric, Coca-Cola, Prudential, and other major corporations have appointed Chief Learning Officers. General Motors tapped the respected former president of its Saturn division, Richard "Skip" LeFauve, to lead its new General Motors University. And at PepsiCo, Vice Chairman Roger Enrico co-designed and now personally leads a leadership development program for up-and-coming PepsiCo executives.

Yet, as noted in *Fortune* not long ago, the Chief Learning Officer remains "a rare bird." Probably less than a fifth of the Fortune 500 companies have created such a role.[7] This leads us to believe that while the door to a more formal strategic role is now open to T&D, training must make more meaningful and tangible contributions to capitalize on the opportunity.

Conclusion

The combination of executives' growing appetite for effective learning, their skepticism about the business value of the training their people actually receive, and their relentless drive to reduce fixed costs has thrust T&D into the corporate spotlight. This constitutes an enormous opportunity as well as a significant challenge to everyone in Training and Development.

Touting the virtues of learning, per se, will only get T&D so far, because business leaders have heard and, for the most part, have bought into that message. They recognize that T&D has the potential to make a significant difference for the business. Now they're waiting for T&D to step up and make such a difference. They're waiting, in other words, for T&D to deliver more unmistakable value.

Keys to Making These "the Best of Times" for T&D

> ➤ Seize the opportunities and accept the challenges posed by the emerging knowledge economy.

> ➤ Challenge T&D to make more relevant, tangible, and accessible contributions to business performance.

> ➤ Remember that training is but a means to business ends.

> ➤ Proactively factor learning and training strategies into overall business strategies.

> ➤ Don't expect executives to give T&D the benefit of the doubt.

2

Missed Connections

When Ed Trolley, a career line manager, was tapped to lead T&D for a Fortune 500 company, he asked each of his new T&D colleagues, "What value would you say our function adds to the business?" Several stared back at him as if to say, "Come again?" A little embarrassed for them, Trolley rephrased his question: "How does T&D help this business make, sell, and distribute products that satisfy customers and earn profits?"

They'd then nod, seem to catch his drift if not his precise meaning, and start to tell him about their work, often with great passion. "Haven't you read the reports?" they'd ask. "We offer thousands of programs around the world. And the evaluations show that participants love the content and the instructors." T&D was stimulating minds, building skills, and making people happy.

That seemed adequate to the folks in T&D, perhaps, but not to some of the company's executives. One told us, "Training here was very program-oriented. Some trend popped up out in the literature, and all of a sudden we were doing a training program in it, even if no one asked for or particularly wanted such training. It was almost as if training was something separate from the business."

Something separate from the business. That phrase speaks volumes. The truth is, T&D has often struggled to find its place in the corporate strategy.

In the chapters that follow, we'll outline how training can move closer to its customers. But for now, let's focus on understanding why savvy, hard-working training professionals so frequently strain to connect with the business executives they serve. Let's consider, as well, how T&D's separation from mainstream business culture often makes it difficult for training professionals to provide unmistakable business value.

Figure 2-1: Where Does T&D Fit In?

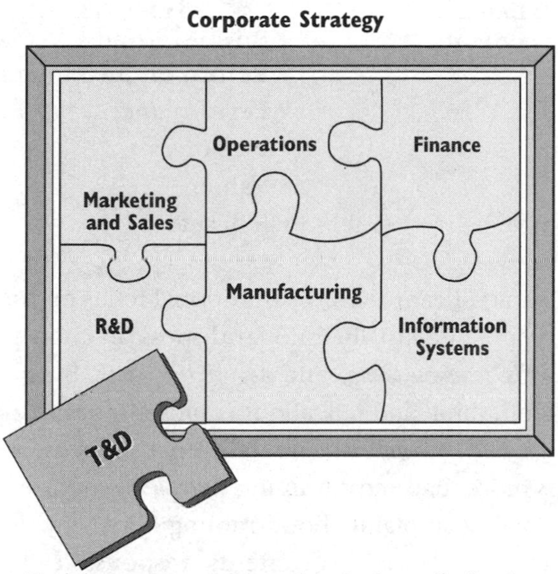

Corporate Strategy

Training and Development hasn't always fit cleanly into corporate strategy.

Roots in Education

The heart of the training mission is to *teach,* and the T&D psyche seems more deeply rooted in education than in business. We believe training's roots in education explain, in large part, why T&D professionals and business executives are often out of sync.

Back when we were in school, students were seldom challenged to find practical applications outside of the classroom for the multiplication tables, spelling words, or poems we studied. In fact, we were immersed in an educational system that held purely practical—that is, "vocational"—education in relatively low regard.

Similarly, T&D professionals sometimes equate learning with mastering content, whereas most business leaders equate learning with improved job performance.

In pursuing its education-based mission, T&D has traditionally approached its work with priorities fundamentally different from those that guide its customers—the business executives who pay for training. The following table sums up the differences.

Training's Traditional Focus Is on . . .	**Business Executives' Focus Is on . . .**
• Training content	• Business results
• Cost	• Return on investment (ROI)
• Skills	• Performance
• Programs	• Initiatives
• Volume	• Value
• Participants	• Markets

Perhaps most significant is T&D's traditional focus on training content. Training people habitually think and speak in conceptual terms like *leadership skills, team building,* and *negotiation skills.* Business people, on the other hand, think and talk about results—*increased market share, improved earnings, profitable growth.* This difference in focus probably irritates executives more than most training people recognize.

"That was a main complaint about training here," says Ken Broker, a Vice President of Texas Instruments responsible for Human Resources in the Materials & Controls division. "Some of our managers even called T&D 'a commodity house.' It was not a compliment."

"That's the case in a lot of places," comments Denny McGurer of Moore. "Ask line managers in most companies about what they get from their T&D—whether it's from internal or external T&D sources—and they'll tell you that most training is 'activity-driven.' It's not tied to any clear business purpose."

Further, T&D has traditionally operated under different premises than does the typical free-market business. We've summarized the different viewpoints in the table below.

Some executives must consider T&D's operating premises less than rigorous. We've encountered more than a few who believe they are held to much tougher standards and are asked to take much greater professional risks than are their counterparts in T&D. Who can doubt that such perceptions further separate T&D from the businesses it exists to serve?

Training's Traditional Operating Premises	Free-Market Business's Operating Premises
• Demand for training is assumed	• Live with risk
• Must operate within budgets	• Must maximize profits
• Sustained by corporate edict	• Sustained by customers
• Fixed cost: Business units pay corporate allocation for training, even if they don't use it	• Variable cost: Customers pay only for services they use
• Job is to convey content, teach skills, build competencies	• Job is to meet customer needs
• Measure success by activity levels (e.g., number of people trained) and budget compliance	• Measure success by customers' success and profitable growth

Demands for More Measurable Results

Measurement is the issue that most clearly illustrates T&D's separation from the business mainstream. The gauntlet thrown down by executives—in essence, "Prove your worth"—has launched training on a veritable measurement crusade. This is evidenced by the torrent of measurement articles in the popular training periodicals and by the overflow crowds that any presentation on measuring training's impact draws at conferences. The training community has taken up the measurement cause with a fervor worthy of Arthur and his knights.

There is, in fact, substantial evidence correlating investment in training with superior business performance. In 1998, for example, the American Society for Training & Development (ASTD) published a report based primarily on a major survey of training practices and expenditures. The sample included 540 U.S. firms, all with 50 or more employees, representing such diverse industries as heavy manufacturing, insurance, transportation, high tech, customer service, and health care. ASTD also drew on the 1995 Bureau of Labor Statistics survey and a handful of other surveys to compile its findings. While ASTD's researchers cautioned that "the evidence at this point is only indicative," not conclusive, they found that "A solid relationship does exist between a company's performance and its work-

Figure 2-2: Bigger Investments, Much Bigger Profits

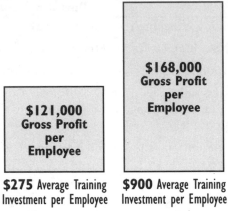

$275 Average Training   **$900** Average Training
Investment per Employee   Investment per Employee

ASTD research showed that companies investing more in training per employee generated an average of $47,000 more profit per employee.

place learning and development practices. Companies that use innovative training practices are likely to report improved performance over time and better performance than their competitors."[1]

Other research published by ASTD correlates investments in training with superior sales and profitability. ASTD sampled 40 publicly traded firms, which they split into two groups according to how much they invested in training. The group of heavier spenders invested an average of $900 per employee in 1996, compared with an average training investment of just $275 per employee for the group of lighter spenders. During the first half of 1997, the companies that invested more in training averaged an annualized net sales per employee of $386,000, compared to just $245,000 in sales per employee for the light spenders. The heavy spenders also earned more than $168,000 annualized gross profits per employee, as compared with gross profits of just $121,000 per employee for those that had invested less in training.[2] Figure 2-2 illustrates the difference graphically.

Another study—"Predicting the Performance of Initial Public Offerings: Should Human Resource Management Be in the Equation?"—found that similar correlations also hold true in newly public firms. The researchers divided a sample of companies that had recently made initial public offerings of stock (IPOs) into two groups: those that made extensive use of HR and training, and those that did not. Nearly 80 percent of the former group survived the challenging years following an IPO, compared with just 60 percent of the latter.[3]

There are reams of such data. Yet measurement remains something of a bugaboo for T&D. Even ASTD, in reporting the research findings cited above, acknowledged: "Despite the growing importance of human capital to companies' survival and success, the measurement of corporate human capital investment—such as workplace training—has been inconsistent at best. The absence of such information makes it difficult for corporate decision makers to make well-informed choices about how much money to spend on training or what types of training to offer."[4]

The training profession has certainly *tried* to provide measures that would satisfy business leaders. As far back as 1959, Donald Kirkpatrick proposed a system for assessing a specific training activity's value to a specific business. This famed "Kirkpatrick model" suggests that training can and should be measured at four levels:

- *Level 1: Reaction*—Did the participants like the program?

- *Level 2: Learning*—What knowledge, skills, and so on did the participants gain?

- *Level 3: Behavior*—Do the participants behave differently as a result of the program?

- *Level 4: Results*—Did the program effect results like costs, quality of work, productivity, and so on?[5]

The Kirkpatrick model is elegantly logical and undoubtedly useful. In fact, it remains the mostly widely accepted framework for measuring training's impact. Our question is, Given all the energy subsequently focused on training measurement, why is a model proposed in 1959 still the standard today?

It is not because Kirkpatrick provided the perfect measurement solution. Anthony P. Carnevale and Eric R. Shultz, writing in a 1990 issue of *Training & Development,* noted, "It's difficult to isolate the beneficial organizational results (that is, Level 4). Most employee training is still evaluated only at the reaction level."[6]

More recently, a Conference Board research report concluded: "Kirkpatrick's approach to evaluation is rarely fully implemented. Only 51 percent of the companies in this study use the Kirkpatrick evaluation model, and they rarely get measures that link training effectiveness to business results."[7]

That's true even of many of the most sophisticated and highly capable training organizations. Oracle's Customer Education division, the world's second-largest provider of IT training, certainly fits that category.

"We've always measured Level 1 in the classroom. We hand out 'smile sheets' at the end of each session, to see what people liked or didn't like about the training experience," says Jackie Stephens, Vice President in charge of Europe, the Middle East, and Africa (EMEA) for Oracle Customer Education, which provides training services to customers using Oracle solutions. Stephens's region alone sold and delivered about $150 million in training services last year.

"For a while now," she says, "we've also done Level 2 measurement, which is built into our courseware. And last summer, we ran our first-ever Level 3 evaluation." Oracle Customer Education conducted a worldwide telephone survey, Stephens explains, contacting customers roughly six months after their Oracle training event to gauge how thoroughly they were applying what Oracle Customer Education had taught them.

"Measurement is definitely a concern of our customers," Stephens says. "It becomes even more of a concern as the transaction size increases. In those instances, we tend to interact with clients at a high level. And people at high levels generally want a clear return on their investments."

When we pressed Stephens on the feasibility of measuring Oracle Customer Education's value out to Level 4, the actual return on investment (ROI), she was candid. "We're experimenting with Level 4 measurement," she said, "but I can't say we've yet isolated the ROI on our training. Oracle Customer Education frequently works as part of a comprehensive IT solution, through which our clients buy a combination of Oracle software, consulting, and IT training. And quite often, we can measure the impact of this *total* Oracle solution. After we work with a client to install a new financial applications suite, for example, we may see their cycle time for closing accounts at year end reduced from three weeks to just five days. But could we strip out the client's ROI on the training component alone?" Stephens gives the question thought. "Perhaps," she ventures, "but only if the client worked very hard at it with us. I don't see how we could do it on our own, do you?"

No, we don't. And when push comes to shove, few business leaders seem willing to work terribly hard to measure training's impact.

Measurement vs. Confidence

This leads us to suspect that measurement has been something of a red herring for T&D. When executives ask T&D for "proof" that training provides good business value, we believe they may really be looking for *confidence*. After all, if executives were confident that T&D was meeting the important and strategically significant needs of the business, would they pound the table and demand precisely measured value? Probably not. Measurement is hard work. It can also be expensive. Executives who are already confident in the returns on their training investments wouldn't want to expend resources "proving" that training is valuable any more than they'd want to waste resources "proving" that safety programs are worth maintaining, or precisely measuring the ROI on their investments in modern telephone equipment.

In fact, we suspect it's not the lack of a workable measurement approach, per se, that blocks many training functions from measuring their ROI. Rather, it is that the traditional training organization was conceived to develop and deliver training content rather than to provide unmistakable business value. Since training often sets its priorities using fundamentally different criteria than those line managers operate by, many of the activities T&D struggles to measure are largely irrelevant to the very people who demand measurement. How can you measure the "business impact" of an irrelevant activity? You can't.

Small wonder, then, that so many competent, well-intentioned training professionals are falling farther and farther behind in their race to keep pace with customers' rising expectations for document-ed value. They have been thrust into the equivalent of the Kentucky Derby, but their mount is more a camel than a thoroughbred. No matter how hard they kick the beast, it will only move so fast.

We believe that what business leaders want most—even those who scream for measurement—is for their colleagues in training to think and act more like business people. Measurement is part of the solution, but it is far from the whole solution.

To think and act more like business people, training professionals must accept that being good at one's craft is important only to the extent that it delivers value to the business, just as advertising copy-writers must accept that they won't be valued for writing fine poetry, and engineers have to understand that they won't be valued for inventing clever but useless gizmos.

Being good business people means understanding the customer's needs. It means consistently translating those needs into learning solutions. And it means ensuring flawless delivery of those solutions, day in and day out. Most of all, it means fitting cleanly into the business strategy and being able to credibly show one's customers—through measurement and through everyday business experience—that they are receiving unmistakable value.

To do all those things well, most T&D organizations—be they internal or external, working in large companies or small—will have to go through a fairly radical transformation. They will have to look forward rather than back. It is time to add a new chapter to the training tradition. It is time for Running Training Like a Business.

Conclusion

Is T&D connected? In many ways it is not. It is distanced from the businesses it serves by its roots in education, by its focus on training content, and by its distinct set of operating premises. And though T&D has worked hard to move closer to the business mainstream, a gap clearly remains—a gap that T&D must close to deliver unmistakable value to business.

Keys to Connecting T&D to the Business

➤ Consider whether T&D fits cleanly into your corporate strategy.

➤ Recognize how training's traditional values differ from those held by most business executives.

➤ Retain the best of training's traditional approach while moving decisively closer to T&D customers' business values.

➤ Make measurement part of a broader strategy to build executives' confidence in T&D.

➤ Encourage training people to think and act more like business people.

3
Running Training Like a Business

Creativity . . . producing through imaginative skill. *Courage* . . . readiness to embrace challenges. *Honesty* . . . speaking the truth. *Realism* . . . adherence to the facts. The ideals to which most people aspire, personally and professionally, tend to be simple in concept. *Living* those ideals day after day, on the other hand, takes great determination.

The approach we advocate in this book—Running Training Like a Business—operates a lot like those familiar ideals. Running Training Like a Business means being simultaneously effective *and* efficient. That's the core of the concept. Here, briefly stated, are the keys to making it happen.

To achieve *effectiveness,* one must:

- Link T&D to business strategy.

- Focus on business issues rather than training content.

- Let customer demand shape T&D's offerings.

- Clarify T&D's business mission.

- See T&D as an enterprise, not as a function.

To achieve *efficiency,* one must:

- Expose hidden costs.

- Aggressively reduce costs.

- Build and maintain reliable systems and processes.

- Operate as a variable cost, not a fixed expense.

- Be flexible and opportunistic in sourcing.

To achieve *both,* one must:

- Measure what matters.

This chapter offers an overview of these basics. Later chapters will provide more details, tools, and examples. Throughout, we'll share experiences and perspectives we've gathered from some pioneers who are now leading their organizations in this new direction.

Link T&D to Business Strategy

Effectiveness begins with understanding what training's customers hope to achieve and dedicating T&D to fulfillment of those goals.

"That takes discipline," cautions Denny McGurer of Moore. "You can't have any of this, 'Hey, there's a neat topic. Let's develop some training!' You have to bring a serious business discipline to everything training does."

Such discipline is conspicuously absent from many training organizations. We've encountered more than a few major companies that maintain hundreds or even thousands of open-enrollment courses, although no one has credibly demonstrated that the courses in the catalog make a meaningful contribution to the success of the business.

Ford Motor Company, for example, traditionally relied on a catalog approach to training. In fact, Ford Learning and Development still offers more than 400 events and seminars for which employees may register, with input from their managers, via telephone or the Internet. "That, in my view, is the past," comments Rolf Woldt, Ford's Worldwide Director of Education Learning and Development. "We receive plenty of positive feedback from participants on most of those courses we offer, because it is for the most part good training. But training participants are just one customer of Ford L&D. We have not spent enough time thinking about our customers who are Ford line managers and Ford executives. It is time we delivered more of what they want and need from Learning and Development."

In short, when you run training like a business, offering training that develops employee skills isn't good enough. The training you provide must also contribute—visibly and substantially—to fulfillment of customers' business strategies.

Focus on Business Issues, Not Training Content

Training professionals and training organizations often define themselves in terms of the content they offer—supervisory skills, sales training, technical training, and so on. We've found, though, that shifting one's focus away from your training content to understanding the *issues* that face the business can open enormous new opportunities for training to deliver value.

An issues mind-set served us well, for example, when the Worldwide Director of Marketing for a major product called a training alliance we'd formed just a year before. Significantly, she did not call with a request for a specific kind of training content. She didn't even mention training. All she wanted to know was, Could the alliance help her division achieve a major gain in sales revenue?

We soon found that this marketing executive had challenged her people to bring in $100 million in sales *beyond* those expected from existing relationships with customers.

As a first step in the engagement, the alliance sent out several staff consultants on a fact-finding mission. What they found from interviews with salespeople and managers all over the globe was that many of the division's salespeople simply didn't have the customized selling tools they needed to meet the worldwide director's challenge. The alliance then worked with the director to formulate a training strategy based not on the content it had available but on the *issue* facing her division.

Once the strategy was set, the alliance took off around the world, reaching most of the division's 46 international branches and presenting issues-focused training in several different languages.

The division subsequently achieved $80 million in incremental revenue—more than enough to make everyone involved positively ecstatic. The team that developed and delivered the training asked the marketing executive how much credit for that sales growth should go to the training initiative. "I'll give you half of it," she said. "No, that's too much," said the team leader. It was a delicious moment, a training manager protesting that a line manager was giving too much credit to training for her division's business success.

The executive and the alliance agreed that the training should be credited for enabling her salespeople to gain roughly $20 million in sales they otherwise would not have won. All in all, a pretty effective return on a total investment (direct and indirect costs) of $375,000.

Let Demand Shape T&D's Offerings

Focusing on issues naturally leads to letting customer demand shape T&D's offerings. Generally speaking, demands for certain types of training will remain fairly constant. But training that runs like a business works tirelessly to offer training that matches new and emerging demands.

"Training's mission here is twofold," explains Paul Earley, Mellon's First Vice President of Corporate Staffing and Employee Development. "First, we provide a core curriculum designed to train individuals in basic skills and core competencies. Second, we conduct ongoing needs assessments across the corporation aimed at making training more strategic and providing training that has more business impact."

Of course, if T&D is going to work this way, it has to stay loose. A significant percentage of its offerings will undergo constant change in response to constantly changing customer demands. Training that runs like a business never settles for what worked in the past. It seeks to be effective in the future.

Clarify T&D's Business Mission

Another hallmark of training that runs like a business is clarity of mission. While remaining extraordinarily responsive to changing customer needs, the training enterprise consciously avoids trying to be all things to all people. A big part of achieving effectiveness, after all, is concentrating your efforts on what's most important to your customers.

For example, The Learning Investment—the training alliance we helped shape at Mellon—has homed in on integrating different parts of the business as its overarching mission. "Banks, at least the big ones, tend to make a lot of acquisitions," notes Allen Roberts, General Manager of The Learning Investment. "Mellon has brought many different organizations together, quite rapidly. It's not surprising that an organization that has evolved in this way has its share of stovepipes and silos. Training will bring an overall view that, frankly, a lot of people around the corporation may not have."

Mike Spurling, Oracle's Director of Internal Training for Europe, the Middle East, and Africa (EMEA), summed it up best: "You want to stake out a well-defined and crucial role in the business for your training organization. You're not just promoting learning. You're promoting learning to make something important happen for the business."

Spurling is working to focus training in Oracle on helping the fast-rising software company to mature as a company, secure its business gains, and sustain its momentum. "Our company became enormously successful in a very short time. We've had 35 percent growth per year with strong margins. That kind of growth totally outstrips structures and policies, not that many people around here have been overly concerned about such things. We've been too busy riding the tidal wave of growth.

"It's only now," he says, "that we're really starting to look back behind the tidal wave and ask, 'Could we be better?' The answer is that we can be *much* better. Right now, there's no consistent approach. That was fine in the early days. We just took the business and kept moving. Now, strategically, we're looking to put the pieces together for our customers, to sell them IT solutions rather than just software. Consistency is becoming very important, and training has to take a lead in creating that consistency, even as Oracle continues its rapid growth."

Arriving at a clear training mission, tightly matched to the needs of a business, can take many months. NatWest, the U.K.'s fourth-largest bank, has been working for nearly a year to carve out a new role for Learning and Development, and seems to have gained substantial clarity on what L&D should do.

"Strategically, customers are looking for a more relational approach from our bank," says Chris Bottomley, NatWest's Director of Human Resources, Retail and Commercial Businesses. "They want this big bank to work smoothly for *them*. However, within NatWest, we have 14 different businesses. Training is going to be a critical part of preparing our businesses to work more closely together for our customers."

That means that training must become much more responsive and much faster than it has ever been before. "If the world changes in six months' time," Bottomley says, "then training has got to change in five months."

By comparison, the training organization at Texas Instruments (TI) Materials & Controls division is still working its way toward a new vision of what it could and should do.

The 4,000 employees of TI's Materials & Controls business in Attleboro, Massachusetts, make custom-engineered controls, sensors, and materials for use in transportation, appliances, HVAC/refrigeration, manufacturing, electronics, and communications. "Texas Instruments is basically an engineering culture. Training here was traditionally very directed," explains Ken Broker, a Texas Instruments Vice President. "Basically, the company would conclude what training people needed and then provide it."

About five years ago, though, Materials & Controls decided to raise the bar. Management declared that each and every employee would get a minimum of 40 hours of training per year. "Well, the company couldn't 'direct' fast enough to implement that much training, and a movement developed to get employees more involved in choosing their own training," Broker says. "People have been feeling very good about this," he adds. "They've come to see training as an important benefit. And the fact that we made this kind of learning commitment to our people has been a point of pride for our company."

That could have been the end of the story. But lately, ongoing change in the Texas Instruments business culture has caused some people in the Materials & Controls division to question the idea of 40 hours per year as a training standard.

"We used to talk about the importance of 'being a player.' That was part of the Texas Instruments culture, and it focused HR on providing a positive work environment," Broker notes. "When viewed in that light, 40 hours training per year for every employee seemed like an ambitious goal. Now, our business culture is more about playing to *win*. That's an important difference. It spurs us to look at everything we do more critically. We ask, How does this build our competitive advantage in speed, cost, and quality?

"Viewed through the new lens of playing to win, the 40 hour standard seems, to me and probably to some others, a bit arbitrary. Wouldn't it make more sense to assess how much training every employee needs and then commit to *that* level of learning investment? We should do what's best for the business, whether it amounts to 20 hours of training each year or 80," Broker contends.

Chances are, it will take some time for Materials & Controls to settle such questions and clarify the training mission. But we feel confident that it will succeed in that endeavor, because it is asking the sort of questions one must ask to raise a fine, traditional training organization to the next level: Running Training Like a Business.

See T&D as an Enterprise, Not a Function

Our tattered copy of *Webster's New Collegiate Dictionary* (Ninth Edition) offers several meanings for the word "enterprise":

- A systematic, purposeful activity

- Readiness to engage in daring action: *initiative*

- An undertaking that is difficult or risky

- A business organization

We like them all! Each describes important elements of what we mean by Running Training Like a Business.

T&D that runs like a business is nothing if not purposeful. It maintains an intense focus on its customers, their issues, and their needs. And it is thoroughly systematic in its efforts to meet those needs efficiently, consistently, and reliably.

When a T&D organization demonstrates the daring to pursue missions that are linked to the business strategy and focused on business issues; when it takes the initiative to tell its customers, "We can help you get where you're going," or even "You *need* us to get where you're going"; when it willingly tackles big challenges, even those that are difficult or risky; then its people quite naturally start to perceive themselves as members of an enterprise rather than as a traditional staff function. And this is a perception to be encouraged. It makes for a training organization that is ambitious, alert, confident, and pragmatic.

"We need people who are prepared to be aggressive and who view training as a business service, not as something in an ivory tower," comments Rolf Woldt of Ford. "Only aggressive, business-oriented people can build the kind of training organization Ford must have in the future." And what kind of training organization is that?

"We can't define yet, in exact terms, how Ford Learning and Development will look in the coming years, but we know for certain what it must *do*," Woldt replies. "Learning and Development leaders will play a consultative role. They will be much closer to the customer. In fact, they will be members of the executive team, an equal partner. They'll know what the up-front issues are, and they'll do ongoing analysis: Is training really required? Then, they will tap into perhaps 20 or 30 small shared services organizations for training, when needed. The whole structure, in its final form, will be geared to providing exactly what's needed to make a difference for Ford businesses."

The traditional training function is rarely geared to provide "exactly what's needed" by training customers. Rather, it is typically

Figure 3-1: Training Positioned to Deliver Its Content

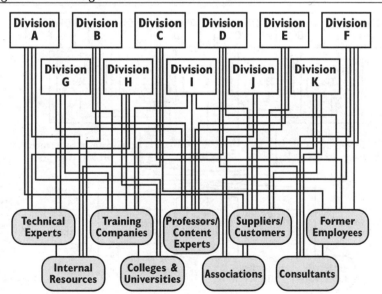

structured to produce training content and then channel that content directly to customers. The absence of a strategic context and
businesslike conduit for training can lead to a tangled web of inefficient transactions, as shown in Figure 3-1.

"We had lots of duplication in Learning and Development,"
recalls NatWest's Chris Bottomley. "We saw that different businesses
were setting up their training activities in less-than-efficient ways and
we felt that, as managers, we had a responsibility to establish more
control over this investment. We had to find a better way."

Contrast training's traditional operating construct with the concept of a training organization expressly designed to be effective and
efficient.

When training is run like a business, none of the traditional kinds
of training providers are excluded. But the new T&D organization—
performing much like a systems integrator for an Information Technology system—makes it easy and efficient for each part of the customer business to access those diverse training resources, as illustrated in Figure 3-2. It also ensures that every training offering is aligned
with the needs of the business.

The training organization depicted in Figure 3-2 is not hypothet-

Figure 3-2: Training Positioned to Address Business Needs

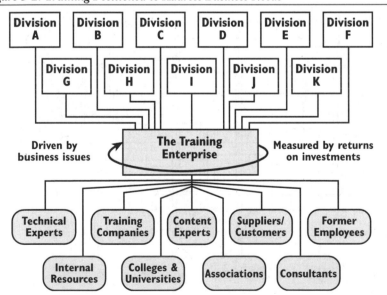

ical. It exists. It is operating or is rapidly taking shape at Moore, Texas Instruments, and NatWest, among others.

At Moore, for example, training is structured and managed as a business rather than as a function. It is led by a General Manager (rather than by a Training Director), and it includes three distinctly businesslike functions of its own:

- *Relationship Management*—roughly equivalent to account management.

- *Capability Development*—creating, procuring, and delivering training solutions.

- *Operations/Support*—administration, logistics, and service.

We often suggest that the training enterprise be conceived using some variation of the "balanced scorecards" now being used by many leading businesses to chart their course to higher levels of performance.

Traditionally, business leaders focused almost exclusively on revenues, profits, and expenses. However, a growing number of executives now realize that while financials tally the results the business has achieved, they reveal little about the inner workings of the business that *produced* those results.[1] A manager who makes decisions based on economic outcomes alone, then, can be compared to a captain who never leaves the bridge. Neither knows just what's happening below decks. That can be dangerous.

Likewise, most training organizations traditionally tracked but a few measures, with similar limitations. "The figures we were using— 'NatWest invests such and such an amount in training' and 'NatWest carried out such and such an amount of training activity'—really didn't mean much to the business," comments Chris Bottomley. "Did it tell us if the *right* people were being trained, or if the *right* training was being delivered? Not at all. Nor did such figures reveal the return we receive on our sizable investment in Learning and Development."

In contrast, balanced business scorecards reveal a whole chain of cause and effect, enabling managers to see (and influence) the various factors that drive success. Figure 3-3 shows one version of the balanced scorecard, which we call the Dynamic Business Scorecard.

Figure 3-3: The Dynamic Business Scorecard

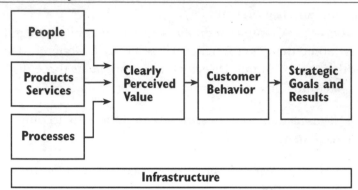

People, working together within *Processes,* create *Products/Services* for customers. When those three core elements of a business perform well, it delivers experiences in which customers perceive clear value. *Clearly Perceived Value* in turn drives favorable *Customer Behavior* (for example repeat buying and referrals), which enables the business to achieve its *Strategic Goals and Results.* To support and accelerate this dynamic, the business builds and maintains an *Infrastructure* of facilities, supply chain, information technology, and so forth.

The Dynamic Business Scorecard can help training organizations, like businesses, measure the key drivers of results, rather than just results themselves. There are other valid scorecard models. But the bulk of our experience has been with the Dynamic Business Scorecard. We have found it customizable to a great many situations and thoroughly applicable to Running Training Like a Business. We will therefore refer to this scorecard often in the pages to come. In Chapter 5, for example, it serves as a framework for assessing the current state of your training function, while in Chapter 7 the scorecard is offered as a tool for organizing the complex transition from a traditional training organization to one that runs like a business.

Here, we'll use the scorecard to briefly introduce the basics of a training organization that is conceived to run like a high-performing business.

The training enterprise is staffed by people with diverse experience and capabilities who play varied roles, yet they all share a *business* mind-set and pursue *business* missions. And because it is cus-

Figure 3-4a: The Dynamic Business Scorecard (People)

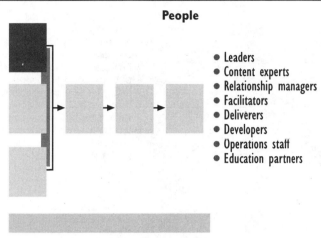

People

- Leaders
- Content experts
- Relationship managers
- Facilitators
- Deliverers
- Developers
- Operations staff
- Education partners

tomer-centered, the training enterprise never hesitates to draw on people from outside the organization to meet customers' needs.

The products/services offered by a training enterprise are comprehensive yet always shaped by customers' strategic priorities. To the fullest practical extent, training products/services are also tailored to customers' business cultures and offered in the shape and form customers prefer.

Training that runs like a business does far more than develop and deliver training. It therefore encompasses many processes, as does

Figure 3-4b: The Dynamic Business Scorecard (Products/Services)

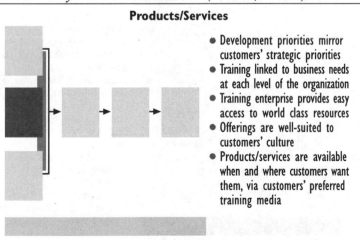

Products/Services

- Development priorities mirror customers' strategic priorities
- Training linked to business needs at each level of the organization
- Training enterprise provides easy access to world class resources
- Offerings are well-suited to customers' culture
- Products/services are available when and where customers want them, via customers' preferred training media

Figure 3-4c: The Dynamic Business Scorecard (Processes)

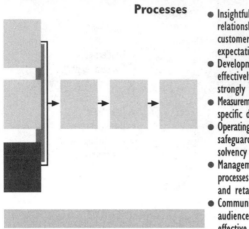

Processes

- Insightful needs analysis and relationship management surface customers' strongly felt needs and expectations
- Development and delivery processes effectively respond to customers' strongly felt needs and expectations
- Measurement processes meet customer-specific demands for perceived value
- Operating systems and budget control safeguard financial efficiency and solvency of the enterprise
- Management and compensation processes consistently attract, develop, and retain top talent
- Communications processes are audience-specific, consistent, and effective

any free-standing enterprise. In Chapter 8 we describe the core processes of a training enterprise in some detail.

The training enterprise—in contrast to the traditional training function—is supported by its own comprehensive business infrastructure. Further, this infrastructure is conceived to be adaptable, so it can flex to meet changing client needs and adjust to the rise and fall of demand for training services. The challenge of building an infrastructure suited to Running Training Like a Business is explored in Chapters 7 and 8.

Figure 3-4d: The Dynamic Business Scorecard (Infrastructure)

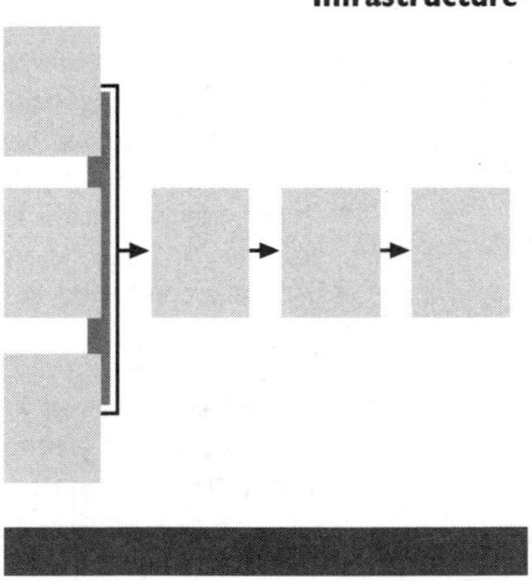

Infrastructure

- Information technology leveraged to help Training enterprise meet more customer needs, more quickly, and more flexibly
- Delivery capacity can flex to meet variable demand for training
- Communications links keep the enterprise attuned with general business as well as training-specific trends
- Facilities and equipment up-to-date and optimized for fulfilling business-driven Training missions
- Supply chain mapped and actively managed for fulfilling business-driven Training missions

Figure 3-4e: The Dynamic Business Scorecard (Clearly Perceived Value)

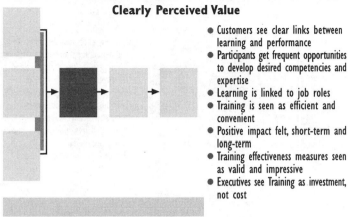

Clearly Perceived Value

- Customers see clear links between learning and performance
- Participants get frequent opportunities to develop desired competencies and expertise
- Learning is linked to job roles
- Training is seen as efficient and convenient
- Positive impact felt, short-term and long-term
- Training effectiveness measures seen as valid and impressive
- Executives see Training as investment, not cost

The training enterprise exists not just to educate but to deliver clearly perceived value, as defined by training's *customers*.

How does the training enterprise know that it has delivered value? Simple. Its customers start doing what every training organization hopes its customers will do.

These positive customer behaviors in turn enable the training enterprise to make ever greater and more tangible contributions to customers' business success. And that is the very dynamic a training enterprise is conceived to create.

Figure 3-4f: The Dynamic Business Scorecard (Customer Behavior)

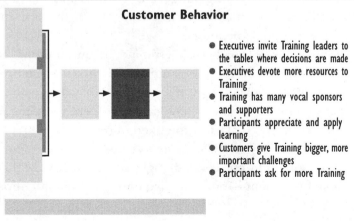

Customer Behavior

- Executives invite Training leaders to the tables where decisions are made
- Executives devote more resources to Training
- Training has many vocal sponsors and supporters
- Participants appreciate and apply learning
- Customers give Training bigger, more important challenges
- Participants ask for more Training

Figure 3-4g: The Dynamic Business Scorecard (Strategic Goals and Results)

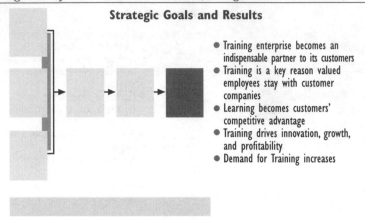

Strategic Goals and Results

- Training enterprise becomes an indispensable partner to its customers
- Training is a key reason valued employees stay with customer companies
- Learning becomes customers' competitive advantage
- Training drives innovation, growth, and profitability
- Demand for Training increases

Expose Hidden Costs

Costs form the very core of most business people's concept of efficiency. Yet few businesses are even aware what their true training costs are because, in most companies' budgets, many training costs are in effect hidden from the line item covering training expenditures. As Figure 3-5 illustrates, hidden costs can be sizable.

Only a fraction of the true costs of training are visible in most organizations. There are no line items in most business budgets for Lost Productivity, Wasted Training Investments, or Lost Opportunity, although these costs are often far greater than the visible costs tracked in traditional training budgets. Executives and training professionals alike are often shocked when they learn the true magnitude of their training expenditures.

"I put together a broad-brush estimate of our training costs," recounts Ken Broker of Texas Instruments Materials & Controls. "I remember thinking how difficult it is to come up with even a rough figure that's accurate. As best we could tell, we were spending about $8 million a year. And that's just the fixed, direct costs. When I held that number up to my fellow managers, I think most of them were surprised. It worked in our favor, though, because they saw that this was a sizable investment—something big enough to pay attention to."

Figure 3-5: Hidden Costs of Training

Moore Corporation was similarly perplexed about how to measure its training costs. "We couldn't really say just what we were spending on training, let alone what we were getting back from it," recalls Denny McGurer. "As business pressures mounted on the company, management began to focus on this major cost over which they had very little control. They started stripping costs out of training right and left. My phone kept ringing, and the voice on the other end kept saying, 'Denny, we need you to cut your budget.' Since I didn't have good information on my actual costs, I was in a poor position to argue."

Aggressively Reduce Costs While Building and Maintaining Reliable Processes

Our first step in working with Moore was to conduct an assessment, a process that we describe in detail in Chapter 5. The Moore assessment documented what the company was actually spending on training, broke that spending down into its component pieces and, most significantly, gauged the business value being derived from those training expenditures. The Moore Learning Alliance subsequently committed, in a contract, to bringing unit costs for training down substantially.

"Reducing costs is just a small part of what we've set out to do in T&D," stresses McGurer. "But when you tell your managers, 'We'd like to reduce our unit training costs by more than a third,' that buys you a lot of goodwill. It helps you win the support you need to address the broader value equation."

Where will the Moore Learning Alliance find the efficiencies required to substantially reduce training unit costs? "We're pursuing strategies that many training functions overlook," explains Mahbod Seraji, General Manager of the Moore Learning Alliance. "We're eliminating duplication. In the past, each business unit dealt with its own training. Now, we are organized to increase our buying power, so we can get the best possible deals. But the real key is we're putting much more reliable T&D systems and processes in place. World-class systems and processes are driving our efficiency, and our effectiveness as well."

Operate as Variable Cost; Be Flexible and Opportunistic in Sourcing

In the preceding chapter, we noted that a fixed cost is one that customers may incur regardless of volume and, in some cases, without receiving value in return. The corporate allocation many business units pay each year to fund the company's Training and Development budget is a classic example of a fixed cost.

Training that runs like a business, in contrast, requires no such corporate subsidy. It operates as a variable cost, one that customers incur only at their own initiative. We believe there are inherent efficiencies in this pay-for-use approach to funding T&D, just as history has shown that there are inherent efficiencies in free-market economies (especially as compared to the notoriously inefficient economy of the old Soviet Bloc).

Making training a variable cost makes especially good sense now that the pace of change in business—and the resulting demands for learning—are accelerating so dramatically. T&D will face enormous and often unprecedented challenges in the years ahead. We've found there's no better stimulus to innovate, improve, and become more efficient than having to *earn* the right to serve customers, each and every day.

The Learning Investment at Mellon, which offers its services on a pay-for-use basis, is a good case in point. "Our training group here works more like a systems integrator than a traditional training function," explains Allen Roberts. "One of our prime tactics is flexibility in sourcing training services. We want to throw presumptions out the window. Instead of automatically running the same program or using the same resource we used last year, we'll search for what will work best. We're looking to deliver more value. That translates into more consistent pricing, for certain, and probably lower real costs for most training services, too."

Measure What Matters

Underlying the entire concept of Running Training Like a Business is a commitment to measuring what matters. So what matters? Effectiveness and efficiency. In business, that's what always matters.

Efficiency measures include familiar figures like total cost, cost per unit, number of participants, utilization rates, throughput, and so on. Most traditional training functions track at least some efficiency measures. However, the consequences of improved or diminished efficiency are minimal. That is why most training functions gather only partial efficiency data and do so only at the end of a quarter, half-year, or year.

Measuring efficiency takes on a much greater urgency when training becomes a variable cost rather than a fixed one. The training enterprise's managers need access to a full complement of operational information in real time so they can make the day-to-day adjustments required to keep a self-sustaining business robust. That is why *Processes* is one of the key components tracked in the Dynamic Business Scorecard.

While efficiency measures are typically associated with your processes, effectiveness measures are more often linked to what your customers perceive and what they actually gain in tangible value. Did they feel they got their money's worth?

T&D's measurement approaches traditionally have included components dedicated to the customer in some way or another, but relatively few break training's customer base into well-defined segments.

Our experience suggests that customer segmentation is essential. Typically, we'll look at the end users of training (the participants), the managers of those end users, and the executives who invest the business's resources in training. We do this because often each of these customer segments wants something quite different from its training investment.

Specifically, the participant generally wants a personally valuable and enjoyable learning experience. The participant's manager or supervisor wants training to help develop competent, capable, and motivated employees. The executive wants to see strong strategic linkage and a clear business return on the training investment. The value of training can therefore mean very different things for each customer segment.

You could find, for example, that your cost-effective learning designs appeal to your cost-conscious executives, but that they alienate or bore training participants. Since participants probably won't learn much from training that doesn't interest them, they won't value it, and neither will their managers, who'll see no improvement in participants' job performance. You might not realize this, however, if you're tracking only executives' satisfaction with your services.

Training needs to meet *all* its customers' needs to have a tangible, lasting impact on the business. When you measure across multiple customer segments—each of which has its own priorities—you see how much more training must do to consistently and simultaneously satisfy participants, managers, and executives. That's good. Training can then move to close those gaps and deliver more real value.

That brings us to a question we regularly encounter: How much measurement is enough?

We say, "The view should be worth the climb." Measurement takes time, effort, and money. So you have to prioritize and decide which measurement mountains are worth scaling. Ask yourself where the investment in measurement is most likely to pay off.

It is generally assumed that the biggest payback from measurement comes from documenting that customers received a good return on their training investments. In fact, measurement is synonymous with ROI in some training circles.

The formula for measuring training's ROI is simple:

$$\frac{\text{Customer-defined value}}{\text{Total training investment}} = \text{Return on investment}$$

However, as we've noted, traditional training organizations generally struggle to find defensible numbers to plug into this formula. How can they accurately fill in the bottom half of the ROI equation—*Total* training investment—when so many of training's real costs are hidden? They cannot. We've also offered several reasons why traditional training organizations may have difficulty calculating the top half of the equation, Customer-defined value. If the training they provide is neither strategically linked nor focused on the customer's relevant business issues, there is little chance their customers will be able to perceive (let alone define) the tangible business value they derive from that training. For these and other reasons, credible calculations of training's ROI are scarce indeed.

In contrast, we've found that when training *is* strategically linked and focused on business issues, customers consistently can define the value derived from that training. This circumstance, coupled with approaches that make training's costs fully variable and therefore explicit, can at last bring credible calculations of training's ROI within our reach, without massive investments in complex measurement systems.

Take the example we shared earlier, in which one of our alliance partners attributed $20 million in sales increases to the impact of sales training.

$$\frac{\$20,000,000 \text{ sales increase}}{\$375,000 \text{ total investment}} = \times 53 \text{ ROI}$$

Sure, the $20 million figure the customer cited was just a rough estimate. But it was an estimate in which she was utterly confident. She had no doubt the training she had bought delivered at least that much added revenue in return. The figure was valid. And it was impressive. That's what mattered to the customer. Why make it anymore complicated?

The second key to relevant, credible, and beneficial measurement of training is to make sure it's "baked in," not "bolted on" after the fact. In our experience, you almost always need to set your measurement strategy beforehand. If you wait until you're wrapping up the training, it's too late.

Training that runs like a business uses a well-defined and time-honored method to "bake measurement in." It approaches each training engagement as a *business transaction*. That is, the training enterprise:

- Clarifies precisely what its customers expect from training

- Negotiates a results contract

- Guarantees customer satisfaction

Expectations, of course, are central to perceived value. Most diners expect far less from a $1.99 fast-food meal than they would from a $200 dinner at a fine restaurant. Similarly, most customers expect less dramatic and immediate business impact from a standard, open-enrollment Word for Windows class than they would for a multi-million dollar, custom-developed, global training intervention. Training that runs like a business never leaves so crucial a value factor as customer expectations undefined. Rather, it carefully maps customer expectations for every business transaction. Some Relationship Managers and Project Leaders use a form to document customer expectations before training begins. A sample customer expectations form is shown in Figure 3-6.

When the training enterprise encounters customer expectations it is prepared to meet or exceed, it works up a results contract that spells out the business results or impact to be gained from the training. A sample results contract is shown in Figure 3-7.

First and foremost, the results contract documents what value will be delivered and at what price. That's wise in any transaction, but doubly so in transactions where value can be subjective. Second, it specifies what the *customer* will do. T&D can do an outstanding job of teaching a customers' salespeople consultative selling skills. But if the participants aren't committed to applying those skills, or if their managers are still badgering salespeople about "closing rates," consultative sales training won't have the desired effect.

Figure 3-6: Sample Customer Expectations Form

Customer/Contact Name:	Title:	Function (Check one): ☐ ADM ☐ INF ☐ SLS ☐ HRS ☐ MFG ☐ SST ☐ MKG
Business Unit:	Tel/Fax:	Cost Center#:

What is the corporate goal? (Check all that apply) ☐ Shift from the product to systems solutions ☐ Growth (profitable) 　☐ Acquisitions 　☐ Alliance 　☐ Internal	What is the business issue?
	What is the business goal?

How is the customer addressing or has the customer addressed this issue? (Current state)

What has worked? What has not worked?

What do people (sales staff, managers, technicians, and so on) need to do differently to meet the goal?

What training and non-training actions need to be taken?

What results are expected and when?

What kind of measures will be used? Explain.

What people resources will be required to deliver those results?

Figure 3-7: Sample Results Contract

Customer Information	
Customer Name:	Contract#:
Title:	Business Liaison:
Business Unit:	Date:
Function:	Project Leader:
Telephone/Fax:	Billing Contact Name:
Mailing Address:	Billing Address (if different):

Strategic Linkage

Corporate Growth: Check all that apply
☐ Internal Growth 2002
☐ Systems Solutions Directive
☐ A-6 Customer Link (non-technology)
☐ Other _____
☐ Other _____

Business Goal
(Summary)

Project Description
(Summary)

Project Pricing

Deliverables	Quantity	Price	Adjustments	Total

Travel, lodging, food, and freight for project billed at cost.

Results Expected

Customer Commitments

Project Evaluation

This project will be assessed immediately following the delivery on these criteria (check all that apply):

- ☐ Customer satisfaction with process
- ☐ Participants' satisfaction with the learning experience
- ☐ Quality of design and delivery (instructor, facilities, materials, communication)
- ☐ Participant learning
- ☐ Project delivered within budget
- ☐ Project delivered on time

Service Guarantee

In the event that a customer is not fully satisfied with our work, impact, or results — for whatever reason — the alliance will do one of the following:

- Provide additional offerings and services at no charge to the customer until such time that the customer deems the work satisfactory.
- Provide a full or partial refund to the customer for fees paid. The level of the refund will be determined by the customer.
- Provide a credit toward future products and services. The level of the credit will be determined by the customer.
- Combine these options in some manner, depending on the circumstances, with mutual agreement between the customer and the alliance.

The alliance requires the opportunity to meet, interview, and assess the appropriate customer representatives for the purpose of full understanding, learning, continual improvement, and development of reconciliation recommendations.

A key feature of the results contract—the service guarantee—is nothing more and nothing less than your promise of 100 percent satisfaction. If the customer is not satisfied with the transaction, for whatever reason, the training organization is prepared to do one of the following:

- Continue the work until the customer is satisfied

- Refund some or all of the customer's investment

- Provide a credit for future products and services

- Offer some combination of the above

We've found that the service guarantee is a powerful tool for building executives' confidence in the value of their training investments. It can turn training benefits from something often perceived as "soft" into something customers view as quite tangible—a money-back guarantee.

We offer this guarantee in virtually every instance. Yet because we work hard to define customer expectations and to create a mutual commitment to the actions set out in a results contract, we've had to make good on it in only a few circumstances, and then at our own initiative.

Conclusion

When you consider all that goes into Running Training Like a Business, you realize just how big a change it would be for virtually any traditional training organization. Still, it is a change worth contemplating.

Businesses have challenged training to become markedly more effective *and* efficient. Working within its traditional operating concept—as a training function rather than as an enterprise—T&D has frequently struggled to respond to that challenge. We anticipate that many more training organizations will soon conclude that, in light of the tasks at hand, many of the old concepts are just too limiting.

There *is* an alternative: Running Training Like a Business. And while this road holds many challenges, it heads straight where training must go to deliver unmistakable value.

Keys to Running Training Like a Business

➤ Bring a serious business discipline to everything training does.

➤ Continually adapt to ongoing change in the business environment.

➤ Promote learning not as an ideal but as a way to fulfill specific business-driven objectives.

➤ Be entrepreneurial—live with risk.

➤ Structure training to provide exactly what is needed.

➤ Divide customers into segments and provide each segment appropriate forms of value.

➤ Document customer expectations.

➤ Write results contracts specifying value to be delivered, at what price, and customers' role in achieving targeted results.

➤ Offer service guarantees.

PART II

Making the
Transformation

The first part of this book explained why we advocate Running Training Like a Business. In Part II, we'll offer our formula for making the transformation from a traditional training function to a training enterprise.

Chapter 4 provides a high-level view of the main phases of that transformation: Assessing, Planning, Installing, and Running.

Chapters 5 through 8 examine the transformation more closely—from our own experience and through the eyes of others already traveling the road to Running Training Like a Business.

4
The Phases of Transformation

Through our work with various customer organizations, we've defined a process for transforming a traditional training function into a training enterprise. The transformation to Running Training Like a Business unfolds in four phases, illustrated in Figure 4-1. Each phase involves certain key steps that, successfully implemented, culminate in outcomes essential to the next phase.

Figure 4-1: The Phases of Transformation

PHASES

We're not saying that this is the only path to Running Training Like a Business. Our experience suggests, however, that a thorough transformation along these lines is essential. In fact, it may take from six months to more than a year for your training organization to proceed through the Assessing, Planning, and Installing phases that bring you to Running, the ongoing phase of operating T&D as an enterprise.

Envisioning this multi-phased transformation from the outset will help you gain the perspective you'll need to maintain an appropriate focus and sustain your momentum over the long haul. In this chapter, we'll offer a high-level overview, based on the transformations in which we've had a hand. Subsequent chapters will explore each of the phases in more detail.

The Assessing Phase

A business assessment of training means far more than confirming the professional competency of T&D, measuring activity levels, or even documenting that skills are being applied on the job. It means assess-

Figure 4-2: Key Steps for Assessing

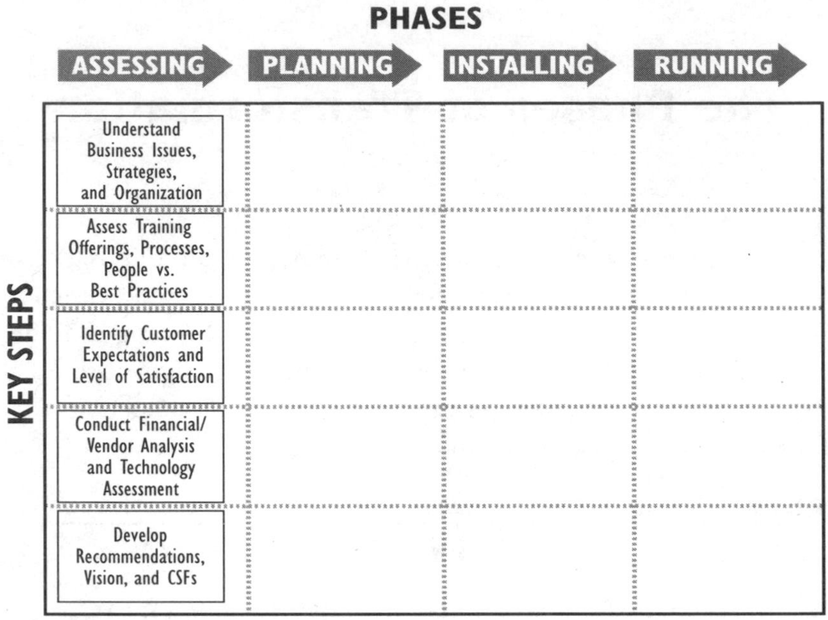

PHASES

ASSESSING ▸ PLANNING ▸ INSTALLING ▸ RUNNING ▸

KEY STEPS

Understand Business Issues, Strategies, and Organization			
Assess Training Offerings, Processes, People vs. Best Practices			
Identify Customer Expectations and Level of Satisfaction			
Conduct Financial/Vendor Analysis and Technology Assessment			
Develop Recommendations, Vision, and CSFs			

ing the strategic and financial return earned on the T&D *investment*.

In the Assessing phase, you'll analyze the strategic relevance, effectiveness, and efficiency of the training organization's offerings, people, processes, and economics. You'll also identify internal and external customers' expectations and levels of satisfaction, develop a compelling vision for the future, and shape actionable recommendations for achieving the vision. Chapter 5 walks you through Assessing, step by step.

Weighing Your Options, Making the Business Case

Although we don't view it as a formal phase of the transformation process, we have identified a crucial interlude between the Assessing phase and the Planning phase that follows. This decision point is illustrated in Figure 4-3.

Assessing generates data-supported options for significantly enhancing training's real business value. Before you move into Planning, you'll want to weigh those options carefully. You'll also

Figure 4-3: Decision Point—After Assessing

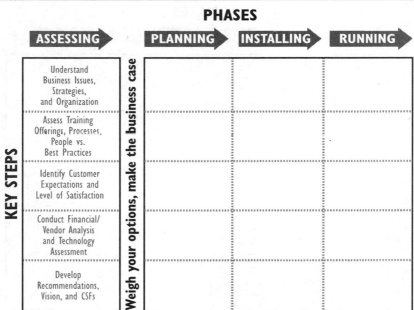

want to use the data and insights you've gained through your assessment to construct a cost-benefit case for Running Training Like a Business. If that business case proves sufficiently compelling, you should press ahead. If it does not, you should either backtrack to Assessing or halt the transformation. Chapter 6 explores this vital decision point in some detail.

The Planning Phase

Once you've clarified why you should run training like a business and what that means for your particular organization, you'll engage in Planning to define the scope, organizational structure, and resource requirements of the new training organization. The key steps in Planning are outlined in Figure 4-4.

Planning should be carried out much as you would proceed in developing any other true business plan and should yield concrete specifications for the training enterprise's key systems and processes, operational infrastructures, training offerings, staffing, communications, marketing strategies, compensation, and business perform-

Figure 4-4: Key Steps for Planning

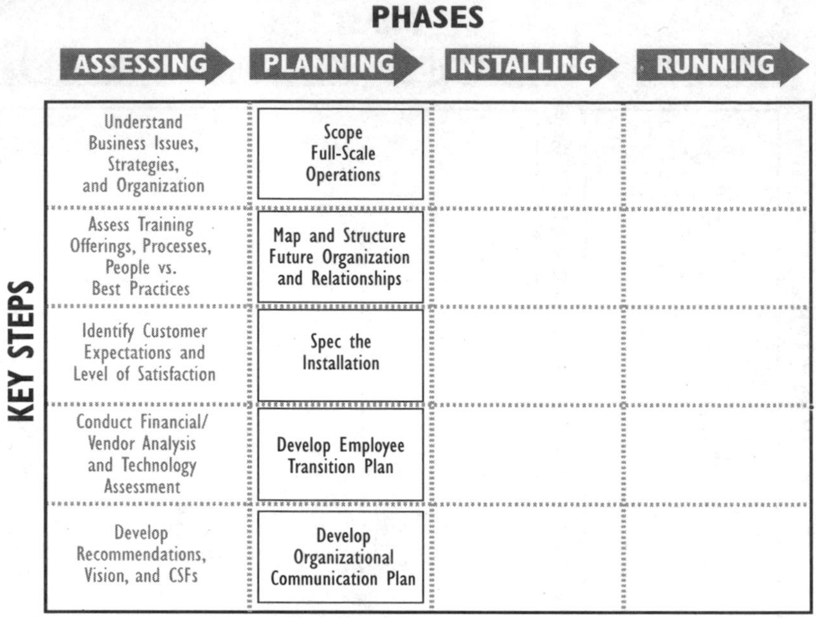

PHASES

ASSESSING	PLANNING	INSTALLING	RUNNING

KEY STEPS	Understand Business Issues, Strategies, and Organization	Scope Full-Scale Operations		
	Assess Training Offerings, Processes, People vs. Best Practices	Map and Structure Future Organization and Relationships		
	Identify Customer Expectations and Level of Satisfaction	Spec the Installation		
	Conduct Financial/ Vendor Analysis and Technology Assessment	Develop Employee Transition Plan		
	Develop Recommendations, Vision, and CSFs	Develop Organizational Communication Plan		

ance metrics. Just as important, Planning details how this new training organization will be installed. Chapter 7 offers an in-depth discussion of Planning.

The Installing Phase

Installing, which begins only after key stakeholders have bought into your plan for Running Training Like a Business, refers to the phase in which you actually develop, beta test, and implement the product offerings, policies, and procedures necessary to meet customer training needs and expectations.

You'll also configure, test, and install your new training organization's key processes and infrastructure; select, align, and train the new organization's staff; carry out an employee transition process for both new and existing employees; and implement your organizational communication process. Chapter 8 walks you through the five key steps for Installing, listed in Figure 4-5.

Figure 4-5: Key Steps for Installing

PHASES

	ASSESSING	PLANNING	INSTALLING	RUNNING
KEY STEPS	Understand Business Issues, Strategies, and Organization	Scope Full-Scale Operations	Develop and Document Product Offerings, Policies, and Procedures	
	Assess Training Offerings, Processes, People Vs. Best Practices	Map and Structure Future Organization and Relationship	Establish Processes and the Infrastructure	
	Identify Customer Expectations and Level of Satisfaction	Spec the Installation	Select, Align, and Train Staff	
	Conduct Financial/ Vendor Analysis and Technology Assessment	Develop Employee Transition Plan	Implement Employee Transition Process	
	Develop Recommendations, Vision, and CSFs	Develop Organizational Communication Plan	Implement Organizational Communications Process	

The Running Phase

By the time you complete Installing, your transformation to Running Training Like a Business is essentially complete. Nevertheless, we include Running as a transformation phase—in part because there tends to be some overlap between Installing and Running, in part as a reminder that a training enterprise never stops changing. The keys to keeping your newly installed training organization vital and successful are outlined in Figure 4-6.

In Chapter 9, we'll look at the training enterprise in action, see how it measures what matters, and explore what it's like to be part of training that runs like a business.

Conclusion

This brief overview was meant to give you a general sense of what's required to turn a traditional training function into a training enterprise. Now that you can effectively envision the transformation, we're

Figure 4-6: Key Steps for Running

PHASES

	ASSESSING	PLANNING	INSTALLING	RUNNING
KEY STEPS	Understand Business Issues, Strategies, and Organization	Scope Full-Scale Operations	Develop and Document Product Offerings, Policies, and Procedures	Lead and Manage the Training Enterprise
	Assess Training Offerings, Processes, People Vs. Best Practices	Map and Structure Future Organization and Relationship	Establish Processes and the Infrastructure	Continuously Improve Operations
	Identify Customer Expectations and Level of Satisfaction	Spec the Installation	Select, Align, and Train Staff	Build Customer Relationships
	Conduct Financial/ Vendor Analysis and Technology Assessment	Develop Employee Transition Plan	Implement Employee Transition Process	Design, Develop, and Deliver Training Solutions
	Develop Recommendations, Vision, and CSFs	Develop Organizational Communication Plan	Implement Organizational Communications Process	Measure What Matters

ready to more closely examine each of its main components, starting with the Assessing phase.

Keys to Envisioning the Transformation

➤ Recognize that this is a multi-phased transformation requiring sustained effort.

➤ Commit to Assessing T&D as an *investment.*

➤ Budget some time for weighing your options and making the business case for change.

➤ Embrace a concept of Planning that will define your new training organization *and* produce practical plans for Installing.

➤ Envision your new training organization running via clearly defined, reliable processes.

5
Assessing: Take Stock of Training

"Assess the training organization." That's not what anyone would call a startlingly new idea.

Many training organizations do assess themselves regularly. But while traditional assessments of T&D may generate reams of data about training, they rarely produce even fundamental data on the *business* aspects of the training organization. How much is actually spent on training annually? What sort of ROI does T&D generate? How does training contribute to overall business competitiveness? What value do training's customers perceive in training services? Many training organizations lack solid answers to such questions, no matter how many times T&D has been assessed.

The assessment we suggest you conduct, in contrast, seeks to bring together, in one place and at one time, the answers to all of these questions:

- What is actually being spent on training and development?

- What value is being returned from this investment?

- How does our training organization compare to others?

- What is the customer's perception of T&D services?

- Where are the opportunities to increase effectiveness and efficiency?

These are questions you must answer to move toward Running Training Like a Business. The key steps for gathering those answers are laid out in Figure 5-1.

Figure 5-1: Key Steps for Assessing

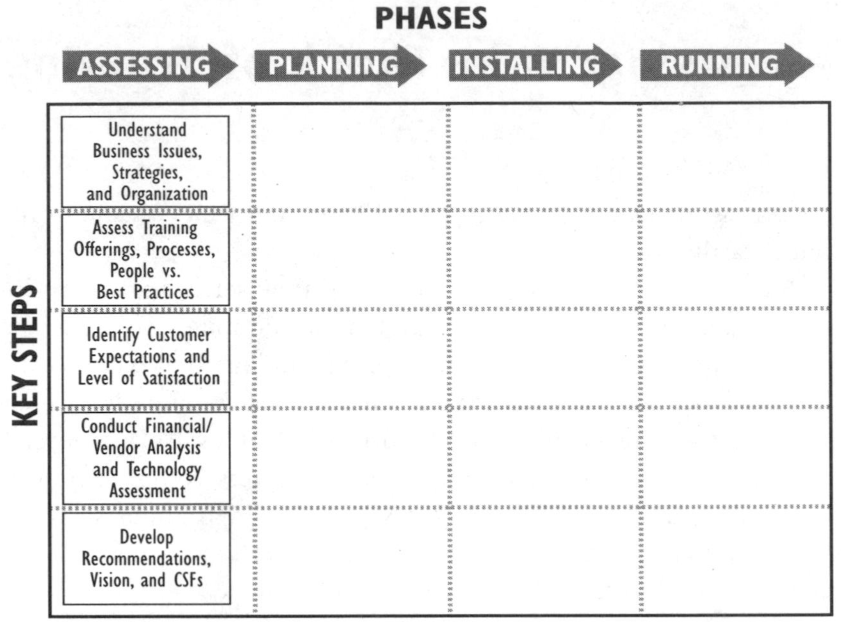

PHASES

	ASSESSING	PLANNING	INSTALLING	RUNNING
KEY STEPS Understand Business Issues, Strategies, and Organization				
Assess Training Offerings, Processes, People vs. Best Practices				
Identify Customer Expectations and Level of Satisfaction				
Conduct Financial/ Vendor Analysis and Technology Assessment				
Develop Recommendations, Vision, and CSFs				

"You absolutely need to start with an assessment of where you are in relation to the business," contends Denny McGurer of Moore. "I've talked to a lot of people in T&D who tell me, 'We've never done an assessment that revealed much of consequence.' I know how they feel. But it could be that they're looking at the wrong things. Our assessment looked at the business facts about our T&D operation, and that put us on a whole new path."

The assessment process described in this chapter analyzes the state of a training organization's offerings, people, and processes—not in the abstract, but in light of the needs of the *business customers* T&D serves. It identifies internal and external customers' expectations and levels of satisfaction, gauges the operating efficiency of training, assesses T&D's linkage to business strategy, and compiles concrete metrics on the real value provided by the training organization. It also yields actionable recommendations that specify the changes required to increase the efficiency of training operations and to make training a more effective strategic lever.

Above all, Assessing as we define it here is an exploration of what is *possible* rather than an affirmation of what is practiced. It is meant to yield bold new visions, to shake things up, and to create new energy for change.

Gaining a Business Context

To assess the value T&D provides in the context of customers' business issues and strategies, you must first gain that context from executives and line managers.

Executives and line managers not only understand the issues, they *define* them. Line managers are also your main source for data regarding customer satisfaction with training. They can identify gaps and give you specifics on your opportunities to improve. Just as important, the simple act of talking with executives and line managers about the possibilities of Running Training Like a Business builds awareness of, and support for, the concept—support you'll surely need down the road.

Unfortunately, you can't expect that everyone will want to sit down with you for a one-on-one discussion. Often, the executives who criticize T&D the most are among the least inclined to devote time toward changing it, at least at first. We're often struck by how much effort is required just to schedule interviews.

So how do you get time on those jam-packed executive calendars? You certainly want to sell the idea of taking part in the assessment. That means thinking about and then communicating specific benefits of participating that should appeal to particular individuals. We have found that this personalized approach is much more effective than giving a standard spiel.

"The concept, Running Training Like a Business, sells itself to a degree. Some managers want to know what that's about," observes Ellen Foley, a Forum colleague who shaped much of the assessment process described in this chapter. "Others need more persuading. The most important thing, we've found, is credible sponsorship. You need to get a few of the right people behind you early on—people in high places. For a business assessment of training, you definitely want the backing of a few executives, line managers, or senior HR managers who have credibility with the line. At times, you'll need them to stand up and say this is serious business, and to open doors that might otherwise stay closed."

Connecting with line managers is always crucial. But we've found that talking with the heads of the various functions is every bit as vital. Managers in charge of Human Resources, Information Technology, Purchasing, and the like have provided us with some remarkably valuable insights. They have also proven powerful allies (or formidable obstacles) to Running Training Like a Business. We've learned, sometimes the hard way, that it is wise to involve such managers right from the start.

"If we had it to do again," a customer once told us, reflecting on the business assessment we had conducted with him a few months before, "I'd devote more time to bringing the functions on board. We actively involved the line managers, but not the function heads. That put their noses a bit out of joint, I think, and well it might. They deserved a say in shaping so significant a change in an area that serves them." He was right. We subsequently worked with him to mend those fences and vowed not to make the same mistake twice.

While getting in the door to talk with all the right people takes a lot of effort, it can also be extremely rewarding. "We spoke with Mellon managers throughout the country," recalls Paul Earley of Mellon. "We'd try to spend at least a day or two in each location, so we could interview people at various levels. What came out of those visits were some pretty consistent issues. But looking back, I'd say one of the greatest benefits was that it opened new lines of communication. We've worked hard to keep those lines open."

We prefer to enter interviews with line managers and executives having already developed at least an approximate picture of the strategic situation.

The chart that follows is the type we often use as a strategic backdrop for our discussions around Running Training Like a Business. It is simple to construct, easy to read, and captures on a single page the ways a business is being obliged to change and is striving to change.

XYZ Corp.	Moving from . . .	To . . .
Market Environment	Stable	Frenetic
Corporate Character	Passive market leader	Aggressive competitor
Attitude Toward Risk	Risk-averse	Risk-tolerant
Product/Service Offerings	Proven	Leading edge
Business Focus	Internal: Efficiency	External: Customer loyalty
Distribution Channels	Few, easy to predict and control	Many, difficult to predict and control

We then use that picture, imperfect though it may be, to shape each interview. Why? Several reasons:

- Basing the interviews on such a picture quickly conveys that this is a different kind of assessment of T&D.

- It conveys to line managers that we're already working to understand the business issues that most concern them.

- Our rough sketch of the strategic situation invites executives to correct, expand, and refine our understanding of their business issues—which is why one conducts these interviews in the first place.

- We can subsequently revise our picture of the strategic situation to demonstrate a thorough understanding of the issues confronting the business.

That last reason often proves most crucial over the long term. In our experience, executives hesitate to consider proposals submitted by any source (not just T&D) that has not demonstrated a thorough understanding of the issues confronting the business. We try to sell our ideas, but we spend at least as much time listening to theirs. The key is to *connect*. That is a crucial step toward credibility.

Choosing Assessment Criteria

We often key our business assessments of training to the Dynamic Business Scorecard introduced in Chapter 3. The thinking behind this approach is easy to explain: Begin with the end in mind. Many respected businesses now use variants of this scorecard to track their performance. If you contemplate one day measuring your training organization as you would measure a business, we suggest you assess the current state of T&D using widely accepted business-measurement criteria. That way, you can compare the status quo directly to the desired future state and identify the gaps.

The Dynamic Business Scorecard, shown in Figure 5-2, is a sound and comprehensive framework for structuring a business assessment of training. Here are the core kinds of data we typically gather for each dimension of the Dynamic Business Scorecard:

Figure 5-2: The Dynamic Business Scorecard

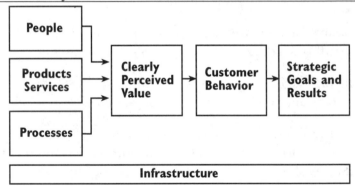

People

- Number of people in the training organization (ratio of training staff to full-time equivalents)

- Resource utilization (percentage of time applied to training activities)

- Satisfaction of training personnel (perception that they are making a difference; whether they find their work rewarding)

Products/Services

- Impact (strategic linkage)

- Results (use of measurement)

- Quality (strength of learning designs)

- Volume (participant hours)

- Flexibility (use of alternative delivery methods, such as the Internet)

Processes and Infrastructure

- Quality of value creation processes (e.g., needs analysis, relationship management, needs assessment, training design and development)

- Efficiency and effectiveness of support processes (e.g., scheduling and registration, vendor management, materials production and fulfillment)

- Use and efficacy of measurement

- Quality of technology infrastructure

- Links to HR, IT, and other company systems

Clearly Perceived Value

- Satisfaction with training work

- Perception of strategic linkage

- Perceived contribution of training

Customer Behavior

- Levels of executive sponsorship/support for T&D

- Investment in T&D (spending by department and division)

- Management cooperation with and support for training activities

- Employee loyalty and retention

Strategic Goals and Results

- Business value/ROI of current training

- Total cost of T&D (as a percentage of payroll, fixed vs. variable costs, internal vs. external providers)

- Average investment per full-time equivalent

- Average unit cost of training

Accessing the Data You Need

If you conduct a business assessment of training, please don't expect the data you need to be laying about like gold nuggets glistening in a stream. Get ready to dig.

Take costs, for example. You might reasonably expect that cost data you'll need will be readily available. After all, businesses run on budgets. They track their costs. As we've mentioned, though, few businesses can readily produce accurate *training* cost data, because so many training costs are hidden in non-training budget lines. For example, few companies track the cost of personnel who are not officially in the corporate training department yet are actively involved in training out in the business units. This is but one of many examples of bona fide training costs that are immersed in other departments' budgets. Purchasing, managing contracts, paying invoices— rarely are these very real training costs included in training budgets or pegged as training expenditures.

Data that reveal the cost of outside training providers may prove especially difficult to pinpoint. Standard Accounts Payable reports blend together all vendors used for everything from training to cleaning the cafeteria. So unless you know the names of every training company, large or small, you'll find it very difficult to cull the data you need from most companies' financials.

Even within the corporate training organization, staff members spend part of their time in non-training activities (for example, company meetings, cross-functional teams, special projects, and so on). That's why we often conduct time studies—literally tracking how training staff members spend their days—so we can factor that non-training time into the true cost of training.

"The data you need usually can be found. But you have to burrow down deep into the organization to get it," summarizes our colleague, Foley. "If you manage to pull together 80 percent of the data you were after, you probably have enough to know what the full picture looks like."

Figure 5-3: Data-Gathering Methods

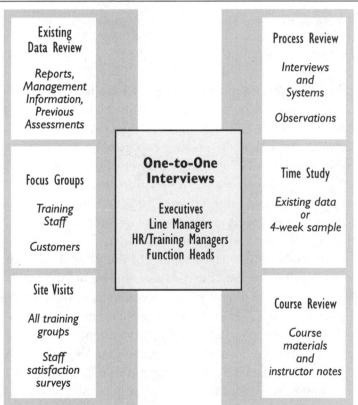

The business assessments we conduct with our customers typically gather and analyze a wide range of both new and existing data via interviews, focus groups, surveys, process mapping, hands-on reviews of materials, and time studies.

Interpreting and Organizing Your Data

One day, you may find yourself gazing at the thousands of data fragments you've gathered, like a paleontologist staring at a pile of bones at the end of a dinosaur dig, wondering how on earth to piece them all together.

Once again, it helps to begin with an end in mind. Assessments almost always culminate with some kind of report. We often structure our assessment reports into four main sections:

- Business situation

- Current state of training

- Recommendations and keys to their implementation

- Financial implications

We like to keep the report document itself slim and focused on presenting the main story. We supplement the report with a separate Data Book that offers all the support data anyone might want. However you approach it, design your report to be *read,* not to make a loud noise when it hits the bottom drawer of some filing cabinet.

Don't be discouraged, either, if you find that many of the data and perspectives you've gathered aren't new. When brought together in one place and viewed in the context of Running Training Like a Business, old data can take on new relevance.

"Previous studies had surfaced many of the same data," explains NatWest's Chris Bottomley. "But this assessment organized all that and more into an end-to-end perspective. We'd never had that. It helped us get our arms around issues that had eluded us for years."

You might expect that compiling an assessment report would be a slow and sleepy affair, but such has not been our experience. In the course of gathering data, we consciously cultivate a sense of new possibilities. That, in turn, builds a sense of anticipation and a healthy impatience. Some people start asking for our report right after the data is gathered!

Throughout the Assessing phase, in fact, you may face trade-offs between doing things properly and doing them fast. If you don't gather enough data, for example, you won't be able to credibly envision how training could and should transition to running like a business. On the other hand, if you string out the assessment process over too long a time, you risk losing momentum. People can easily forget what you're up to.

Cultural differences may also be a factor. We've found, for example, that in companies that are relatively comfortable with risk, people don't mind a few mistakes, as long as you keep moving the process forward at a rapid clip. In other places, though, not doing something "properly," "appropriately," or "correctly" is viewed as a weakness. Every situation is different. The key is to be attuned to your environment and exercise your judgment.

The financial data will likely draw the most attention, interest, and scrutiny from the business decision makers who review your findings and respond to your recommendations. Anytime a piece of financial data doesn't make sense to us, we check it out because, somewhere down the line, some sharp-eyed executive will probably ask us to explain it.

We also focus on the financials because they are the linchpin. You need all the other assessment data to show that you understand the business issues and that you've gained exceptional clarity about the inner workings of T&D, but the financial data is what lets you speak to executives about training in *business* language. You can say things like, "We're spending 300 percent more on training than our nearest competitor. Are we getting 300 percent more value?" You can talk about annual training costs per person in accurate, real-cost terms. And you can make a rock-solid business case for change.

What kinds of data would you see in a business assessment of training? The specific sample findings presented in Figure 5-4—genericized from various reports we've compiled—should give you a sense of what you might want to report, and why.

Figure 5-4: Sample Assessment Findings

Findings re: the Business Situation should summarize the headline issues facing the business, convey customers' perceptions about T&D's potential to impact those issues, offer telling indicators of the reality vs. that perceived potential, and offer some tangible measures of the perceived value currently provided by T&D.

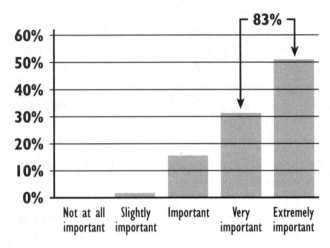

Your Executives See Training as Vital to Business Success

Business Imperatives

- Grow the business through customer focus and differentiation
- Deliver excellent service quality through operational effectiveness, database management, product design, and seamless multi-channel delivery
- Create a proposition that customers value and pay for, adding value through wider lifestyle and personalized services

If Training Were a Business
It Would Be Losing Market Share

Your Line Managers Feel Distanced From T&D Decision Making . . .

- Most do not know what is being invested
- Limited perception of training's business value
- In the main, T&D is viewed narrowly:
  - Technical skills
  - Personal development
  - Management development
- T&D is perceived as an event or activity, *not* an integral part of business operations

Figure 5-4: Sample Assessment Findings (continued)

Findings re: the Current State of Training should describe the kinds of train-
ing activity going on in the business, report existing efforts to measure train-
ing's value, provide indicators of training's effectiveness and efficiency, and
draw clear comparisons with relevant benchmarks.

Volume: Participant Mix

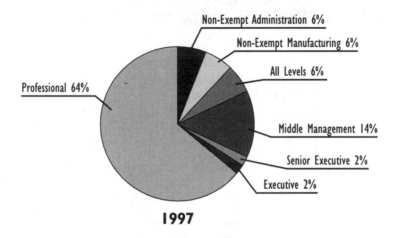

1997

Measurement

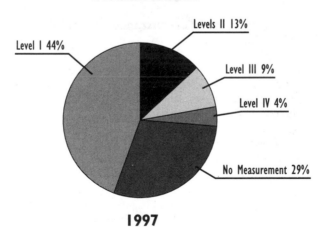

1997

Strategic Linkage

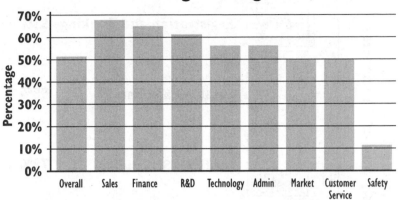

Benchmarks

Cost as % of Payroll

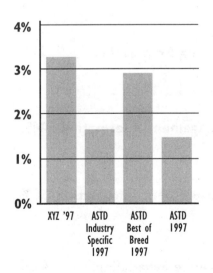

Benchmarks

Training Days/Employee

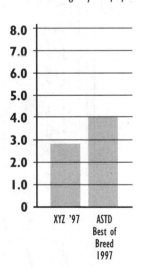

Figure 5-4: Sample Assessment Findings (continued)

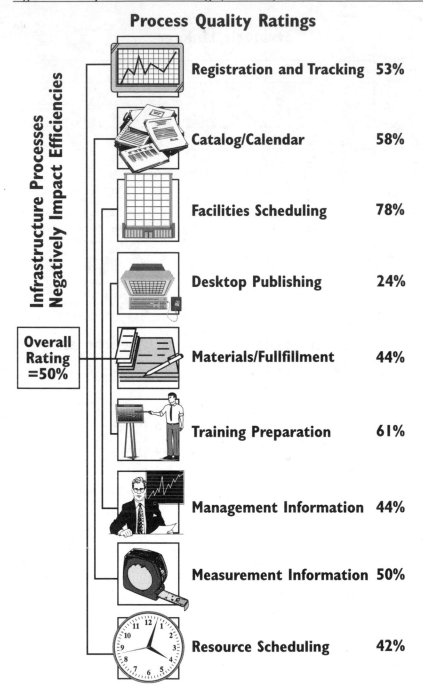

Process Quality Ratings

Registration and Tracking 53%

Catalog/Calendar 58%

Facilities Scheduling 78%

Desktop Publishing 24%

Materials/Fullfillment 44%

Training Preparation 61%

Management Information 44%

Measurement Information 50%

Resource Scheduling 42%

Infrastructure Processes Negatively Impact Efficiencies

Overall Rating =50%

The recommendations you offer should do more than advocate change. They should paint a picture, in broad strokes, of how the suggested change might unfold, and address what types of investments would likely be needed to implement your recommendations.

Recommendations/Keys to Implementation

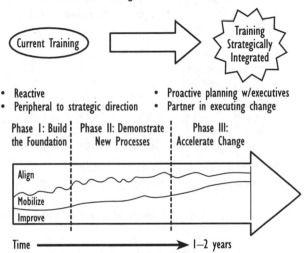

Requisite Investments in Infrastructure Process

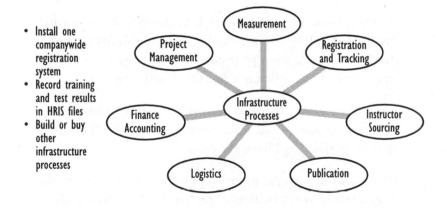

Figure 5-4: Sample Assessment Findings (continued)

When you've completed a true business assessment of training, you can credibly project the potential returns—in hard business terms—to be gained from investing in your recommendations.

Financial Implications
Training Investment: Current vs. Proposed

	Current	Proposed	Delta
Staff	$11.4	$6.5	$(4.9)
Occupancy	7.1	3.0	(4.1)
Technology Support	0.8	1.1	0.3
Outside Content and Materials	11.1	9.8	(1.3)
Other Costs			
Allocated	0.6	0.4	(0.2)
Direct	9.0	8.1	(0.9)
Total Annual Spending	$40.0	$28.9	$(11.1)
Training Days	100,000	100,000	
Cost Per Training Day	$400.00	$298.00	$(111.00)

Annual Savings of $11.1 Million

Shaping the Recommendations

Naturally, the recommendations you make must flow from the data you gather, which means they will be very situation-specific. Still, we can suggest some general guidelines. Strive to make your recommendations:

- *Insightful*—Don't restrict yourself to the face value of your findings. Explore and articulate the implications of the findings, as well, from your customers' perspective. Offer recommendations that address those implications.

- *Transformational*—Draw stark contrasts between what *is*—the current state—and what *could be*—the possibilities for Running Training Like a Business.

- *Predictive*—Be specific in projecting the future state. Avoid vague terms like "excellence" or "world-class" (use such terms only if you can clearly and tangibly define them).

- *Prioritized*—Most executives are interested in costs, strategy, and people. Our recommendations often address those areas first.

- *Comprehensive*—A business assessment of training covers broad territory. That scope should be reflected in the resulting recommendations.

- *Crisp*—Get straight to the point. Be clear. Make it interesting.

Communicating Your Findings

Hallelujah! Your assessment team has traveled far and wide, knocking on executives' doors, conducting interviews, and swimming through the issues that pervade the business. You've led focus groups, analyzed survey data, dug through files, reviewed countless courses, and conducted detailed time studies. You've wracked your brain through late nights, figuring out just what it all means—and just what it *could* mean—for the future of training. You've run down the facts. Double-checked your figures. Compiled your report and shaped your recommendations. Now, at long last, you're ready to communicate your assessment findings.

That is cause for excitement. Still, you probably shouldn't expect everyone to welcome your news with open arms. In fact, you may feel some tension in the air. You need to be sensitive to the full range of feelings the assessment findings may stir.

"I was on the business assessment team, but I still suffered a bit from nerves now and again as we went through the process," says one veteran of NatWest Learning and Development. "Your value to the organization will be reflected in those findings. You just have to remember that this is actually a healthy thing to do. It's easy to react to conclusions you don't like by challenging what's said, or by thinking of excuses. We tried to focus on turning what was sometimes negative feedback into a positive."

At Texas Instruments Materials & Controls, there was quite a bit of concern about how the training organization would react to the assessment report, so we decided to present our findings to them first, even before discussing the report with the senior management team. The initial reactions from the training group were clearly defensive. From their body language, you'd think they were sitting through a tax audit. But over the course of our presentation, we started to see heads nodding up and down in agreement with our findings and conclusions. At the end of the presentation, one of the training people offered this comment: "The senior team will understand what you're saying. You're using their language—*variable cost, strategy, value*—that's how they talk. And you're talking about training in that context, *their* context. That'll help them see that these issues really are important."

It seems that veteran trainer was something of a prophet. Our next presentation was to the Materials & Controls leadership team. "I watched the group's reaction as each finding went up on the screen," recalls Ken Broker of Texas Instruments. "They'd take it in, then start talking to each other. Sometimes it was like the people up front, presenting the findings, weren't even there. And that pleased me. It meant that these assessment findings really spoke to our executives. That's why they triggered so much discussion among them. I'd say it was among the most active and productive discussions we've had."

One major insight from that discussion was consensus among M&C's top managers that, although the division had long invested heavily in T&D, they did not particularly value training, because they felt that it was not very connected to the business. "Our assessment showed that our training operations are actually pretty efficient, but not as effective as they could be," Broker summarizes. "It's like something you'd buy on sale because it's a bargain. But when you get it home, you think, 'Why did I buy this? I don't need it.'" The big opportunity to build unmistakable value for training at M&C, Broker and his management colleagues have decided, will be found in effectiveness. Their main goal is to increase training's impact on revenues and profits.

We've found that executives are often especially intrigued by benchmark comparisons. It's easy to see why. Business people tend to be competitive. It really stirs them up when they hear that, in certain regards, their business is less efficient or less effective than are certain others—particularly others in their industry.

Our assessment findings often compare a particular business's training data to relevant benchmarks, such as the averages documented, and periodically updated, by the American Society for Training & Development, shown in the table below.

Metric	ASTD Benchmarks
Ratio of training staff to total employees	1:315
Training expenditures as a percentage of payroll	2.88%
Training expenditures per employee	$1526
Average training days per employee	4.0
Average cost per training day	$3.82
Training expenditures as a percentage of revenue	.52%

It's important to keep in mind, though, that benchmarking numbers are only relevant in the context of value. If you are spending just $1 on training but getting no business value in return, then you are overspending. If we could match comparisons of training investment with some corresponding comparison of the value subsequently realized, the contrasts would be far more telling. Unfortunately, there's precious little benchmark data on training ROI. Not yet, anyway. We're trying to change that.

One key lesson we'd draw from our experience is that no one or two findings are likely to convince anyone of anything, at least not with the conviction required to transform a traditional training organization into a vibrant training enterprise. Rather, it is the holistic quality of a well-executed business assessment that people find compelling. They respond to the combination of information and insights that, when brought together, point to a new direction. That combination then, truly is what makes a business assessment a success.

"We arrived at a point where we could lay it all out for NatWest's executives," says Chris Bottomley. "We'd conducted a thorough and credible review. We'd shown what NatWest was actually spending and how little we could say, for certain, we were receiving in return. And we convinced them, beyond doubt, that there's real value to be had from training *if* you get it right."

Conclusion

In summary, here's what you get in return for all the hard work that goes into Assessing, as described in this chapter:

Credibility—You're on your way to winning over line management. You've armed yourself with the strength of credible data. And you've earned the right to talk strategy with the people who run the businesses.

Clear vision for the future—You now have a clear alternative to traditional approaches to running training. You can point to another way: Running Training Like a Business.

Clear action steps—You've spelled out, in considerable detail, what must be done to fulfill the vision.

Data for the transformation—The baselines are established. You know your relative strengths as well as your weaknesses. You understand your training organization as you never have before.

And don't forget the intangibles:

- Increased awareness of the power of learning

- Increased awareness that *training* decisions are critical *business* decisions

- The satisfaction of having the integrity and courage to look squarely at what you do and say, "We can do better."

In most organizations, this in itself is a big step in the direction of moving from a functional to a business orientation. Assessing T&D from a comprehensive business perspective reminds everyone—training professionals and line managers alike—that training can and should be an integral and entrepreneurial part of a successful business.

Keys to a Sound Assessment

➤ Involve key stakeholders early on.

➤ Create a strategic picture of the business.

➤ Be sensitive to company culture and politics.

➤ Assess training against respected business measurement criteria.

➤ Dig deep for data.

➤ Bring order and insight to the data.

➤ Balance speed and process.

➤ Let research determine answers.

➤ Make recommendations transformational, predictive, prioritized, comprehensive, and crisp.

➤ Have empathy for your audiences.

➤ Communicate the whole story.

6

Post Assessment: Weigh Your Options, Make the Business Case

◆◇

In the last chapter, we advised you to assemble your assessment data into a gripping story of what training is, could be, and should be for the businesses you serve. Now it is time to weigh your options for fulfilling that vision, and to make the *business* case for pushing forward on that course.

Figure 6-1: Decision Point—After Assessing

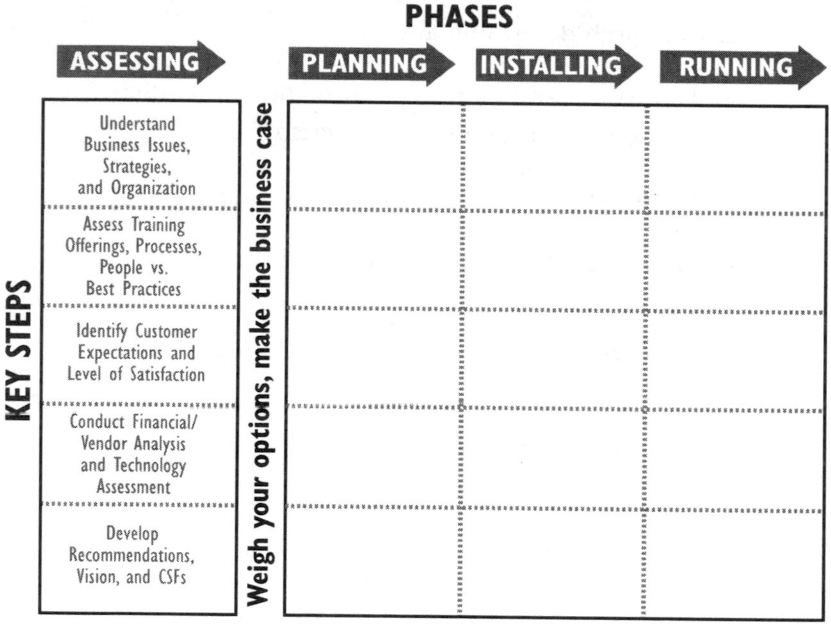

Of course, your business assessment of training *could* indicate that you should do nothing. We've said it before: Running Training Like a Business is not for everyone.

When is it wise not to attempt Running Training Like a Business? When your assessment reveals findings like these:

- T&D is already as effective and efficient as its customers want it to be, now and in the foreseeable future.

- Few key individuals seem excited about or even open to the prospect of Running Training Like a Business.

- Signs suggest that your organization is simply not ready to pursue the transformation required to create a training enterprise.

A decision to maintain the status quo does not make your assessment a failure. You will have gained many valuable and applicable insights from the experience, and you will have systematically explored possibilities that no business should overlook.

Options for Pursuing the Transformation

If your assessment suggests that you should move toward Running Training Like a Business, you'll want to spend some time weighing your options for pursuing the transformation. Our experience suggests that there are three ways you might go:

- Make a strategic investment in reinventing T&D

- Outsource selectively

- Form an Insourcing Alliance

Each approach entails comparable trade-offs, and all require a substantial effort. Which option is best depends entirely on your goals and situation. In the following sections we'll review some of the main advantages and drawbacks of each option.

Make a Strategic Investment in Reinventing T&D

There are impressive precedents for this approach. In 1985, as Motorola was battling for its life against seemingly invincible, quality-obsessed Japanese competitors, CEO Robert Galvin committed 1.5 percent of payroll to training and to establishing a new corporate education arm—the now-famous Motorola University. Motorola today spends closer to 4 percent of payroll on education. Not coincidentally, most observers agree, Motorola won the Malcolm Baldrige National Quality Award in 1989. More important, its products won a reputation for superior quality, and its profits increased nearly four-fold, from $499 million in 1990 to $1.8 billion in 1995.

General Electric's training organization is equally celebrated. When Jack Welch became CEO in 1981, a period of austerity in GE, he spent $45 million on new buildings and other physical improvements to the company's Crotonville, New York, executive education center. Welch championed "action learning"—teaching the skills of solving business problems by having managers solve real problems while working in teams at the center.[1] Welch's continued active support of corporate education is widely regarded as a key to his successful transformation of General Electric, which is now very profitable as well as standing among the world's most admired corporations.

Making a strategic investment to reinvent one's training organization offers several inherently appealing advantages. The business gains a clearly defined, company-based T&D function capable of advancing the companywide strategy. A reinvented internal training organization also maintains an insider's insight into the corporate culture. With sufficient resources, it can make significant contributions to business success, as have the reinvented training organizations at Motorola and GE.

To pursue this option, you'll need to dedicate a team to reinventing T&D. (This is not a part-time job.) Further, the transformation to Running Training Like a Business demands abilities that range far beyond learning and training expertise. The team tasked with reinventing T&D should therefore be cross-functional and should encompass very strong project management expertise, outstanding leadership abilities, sophisticated technological know-how, and proven operational management skills. It should also be representative of the organizations T&D will serve to ensure that the transformation stays attuned to the needs of training's customers.

Credibility with senior management is another vital consideration. To enhance T&D's effectiveness as did Motorola and GE, you'll need the active and sustained support of strong senior sponsors. Finally, your top managers must be prepared to make substantial financial investments in transforming T&D.

Outsource Selectively

Outsourcing is the fastest way to transform a training organization. The Outsourcing Institute defines outsourcing this way: "Transferring primary responsibility for an area or service and its objectives and results to an outside provider for a long-term agreement."[2]

As with making a strategic investment in reinventing T&D, there is ample precedent for outsourcing, but it is more a general business precedent rather than one pertaining specifically to T&D. As Figure 6-2 illustrates, outsourcing of Information Technology, physical plant maintenance, customer service, and other functions is rapidly becoming commonplace. Research conducted by the Yankee Group found that 90 percent of Fortune 500 companies have outsourced at least one major function.[3]

Figure 6-2: U.S. Outsourcing Expenditures

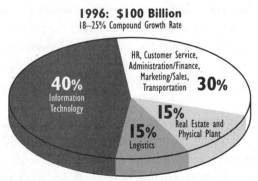

1996: $100 Billion
18–25% Compound Growth Rate

40%
Information
Technology

HR, Customer Service,
Administration/Finance,
Marketing/Sales,
Transportation **30%**

15%

15%
Real Estate and
Physical Plant

15%
Logistics

Businesses have found outsourcing a sound approach for increasing the effectiveness and efficiency of a variety of functions. Outsourcing also allows businesses to focus on developing their own core competencies. Source: The Outsourcing Institute.

Why has business embraced outsourcing? The Outsourcing Institute cites the following top ten reasons:

- Reduce operating costs

- Improve company focus (focus on core competencies)

- Gain access to world-class capabilities

- Accelerate benefits of reengineering

- Share risk

- Free non-capital resources

- Make capital available

- Cash infusion

- Resources not available internally

- Function difficult to manage

While more than a third of the training services consumed by businesses is now supplied by outside providers,[4] this is not outsourcing as defined above, as few businesses have turned *primary* responsibility for T&D over to outside providers.

The prospect that some businesses might transfer primary responsibility for T&D to outsiders—truly outsourcing training—has stirred a spirited debate in training circles. A recent *Training Magazine* article explored the controversy from both sides. This was how the author summarized the points in favor of outsourcing T&D:

> Why outsource the training function? The argument goes like this: A training department is permanent, embedded overhead that costs a company every minute of every day. Ideally, an outsourced function costs only when you use it. Such an arrangement is supposed to leave a company with a low unit cost on its product and more cash available to deploy quickly elsewhere as needed.[5]

To that summary of the pros of outsourcing T&D, we'd add that accessing specialized, world-class training expertise and freeing the business to focus on its own core competencies appeal to many business leaders.

"If you're not an Arthur Andersen, a Forum, or a Harvard, your core competency is not training," says Denny McGurer of Moore. "Moore provides business communications services. That's where we want to invest our time, intellect, and capital. But a top training provider is going to spend millions researching and developing training solutions. They're also going to go out and get the best instructors in the profession. Because if their training capabilities are sub-par, they're out of business."

To summarize the concerns some have voiced about outsourcing T&D, we'll again quote from the *Training Magazine* article:

> The training arm of the company is a major change agent and is one of the key ways you can get improved human performance. . . . Outside suppliers don't know the corporate culture or language, don't understand the nuances, don't know the hot buttons. . . . It's hard for vendors to understand what's going on in a corporation unless they're living there.[6]

Some of our own customers have voiced similar reservations. "Outsourcing basically means you hand over a job to another party," notes Mike Spurling of Oracle. "You might have very tight service-level agreements, but you're still handing responsibility over to somebody else. Because development of your people is the future of your organization, I wouldn't trust outsource providers with full responsibility for training."

Without question, outsourcing T&D would be considerably more complicated—and probably more risky—than outsourcing your copy room, cafeteria, or janitorial services. To run a cafeteria or clean the building, you don't need to understand the strategy of the company, because you can provide the expected forms of value without making direct contributions to fulfillment of that strategy. The Training department, in contrast, must be inextricably linked with what's going on in the business. That is the only way T&D can consistently provide it unmistakable value.

We have seen at least one organization succeed with outsourcing selectively, while keeping primary responsibility for T&D in-house. (Some experts call this method "out-tasking," to distinguish it from total outsourcing.)[7]

"We've formed what we call an Alliance Network," explains Madeline Fassler, Director of Learning for the Medical Care Program at Kaiser Permanente in California. "It is a network of vendors whom we expect to work not only with us but with each other."

The training needs in Kaiser Permanente are so diverse, Fassler and her colleagues reasoned, the training competencies required will often shift dramatically from one learning initiative to the next. "I wanted very competent instructors," Fassler says, "but with variable cost and maximum flexibility. We need to be able to scale down sometimes, then bring our training capacity back up to high levels in very specific areas on very short notice. So we worked out an arrangement with contract instructors from a local vendor. Forum provides us with a consultant who resides with us. She trains and monitors the contract instructors to deliver Forum programs that have been tailored to meet our needs. Forum consultants also supplement our training management team. They coach along with some of our managers, especially to lend facilitative and skill reinforcement expertise, a base of competence that we couldn't find in some pockets of our organization."

We believe this sort of innovation is almost always appropriate and often vital. It seems all one hears about these days is how fast everything is changing. In the midst of all that change, should we assume that the standard approaches—the ones we've all heard of—will go on being the best options available? No. It isn't logical. The logical approach is to engage in experimentation. And the Alliance Network at Kaiser Permanente of California is an experiment that is succeeding.

Form an Insourcing Alliance

In addition to reinventing T&D from within and selectively outsourcing training services, we've found a third strategy worth considering: Form an Insourcing Alliance.

To form an Insourcing Alliance, you bring a partner *inside* your company, merging the best of your existing T&D staff with those of the external training resources to form an entirely new organization. This new organization, the Insourcing Alliance, replaces the former T&D function while retaining the experience and knowledge base accumulated by the current T&D organization. Virtually all of our experience transforming traditional training functions into training enterprises has employed some version of insourcing.

Illustrated in Figure 6-3, the Insourcing Alliance is an unconventional business organization that simultaneously relies on, and is thoroughly integrated with, two sets of systems—those of the company it serves and those of the external training provider(s) chosen to be the Insourcing partner.

Figure 6-3: The Insourcing Alliance

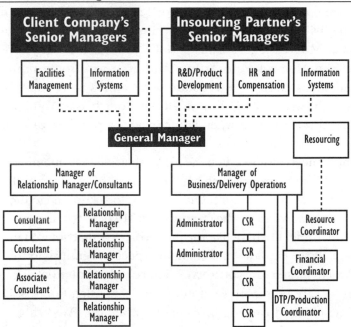

The Insourcing Alliance is housed within the customer company so it can shoulder *primary* responsibility for training. Unlike the traditional training function it replaces, however, the alliance is run like a business, rather than as a corporate function. Alliance personnel search for opportunities to provide value through training, propose to provide services, negotiate agreements for the work, deliver the work, and satisfy the customer.

In the alliances we've formed to date, the new training enterprise is often somewhat smaller than the former T&D function. Yet, by drawing extensively on third-party resources, the alliance brings a broader range of capabilities to the business.

At Moore, roughly 40 percent of the Learning Alliance staff was drawn from the former T&D function. About 20 percent came from Forum. The rest were recruited from the outside.

"Each background has its pros and cons," observes General Manager Mahbod Seraji, who was with Arthur Andersen before taking his position with the Moore Learning Alliance. "Our Moore veterans bring a context—an understanding of the culture, business issues, and history of the company—that is absolutely critical. At the same time, that perspective can work against you. It's only natural that they will harbor some presumptions that 'this is the way we do things at Moore.' The Forum people, too, have a 'way to do it.' I came from Motorola and Arthur Andersen with some pretty hardheaded ideas of my own about what works and what doesn't. Fortunately, we're aware that we all have our biases. You have to be flexible. You learn a lot when you consider a problem or issue from different perspectives."

One concern we've often heard is that alliance members drawn from the training provider will have an unhealthy bias toward their own company's training solutions. Our policy is to acknowledge the validity of this concern. Were we the customer, we'd worry, too, that an insourcing partner might behave like the proverbial fox that got into the chicken coop. So we know we must remain especially sensitive to this issue.

"Which master do you serve? There's the potential for that to become a sore point, but we don't let it," says Allen Roberts, General Manager of The Learning Investment at Mellon. "We bring options: from Forum, other vendors, training that's created within Mellon itself. Less than 40 percent of the training provided by The Learning Investment last year was made by Forum. We respond to the demand of the bank's businesses. You can't do that consistently if you're busy stacking the deck."

NCR issued a Request for Proposals (RFP) in May 1998 that specifically sought an "outsourcing/insourcing" partner:

NCR expects a high quality, cost-effective employee development solution from a third-party supplier which will allow leveraging of relationships, buying power, expertise and experience
which will fulfill NCR's business needs. . . . NCR expects the
supplier to maintain at least one person on-site at NCR's headquarters in Dayton, Ohio, to manage the relationship and continuously assess and fulfill NCR's business needs. NCR expects
the supplier to absorb NCR employees currently dedicated to
this function. . . ."[8]

"We were spending about 6 percent of payroll in all kinds of training, including tuition assistance," explains George Brennan, Vice
President in charge of NCR University. "We're going to trim that figure to 3 percent within the next year or so.

"At the same time, we need for learning to have a much more
direct impact on our business goals, especially our revenue goals,"
Brennan says. "NCR is pursuing a fundamental shift in strategy, from
selling technology products that come in boxes to making more
'solution sales.' That's a big change for all our customer-facing
groups—for everyone, really. We'll have to get better at solution
sales, at consulting, at fixing hardware or software problems the first
time . . . you name it. There's plenty our people need to learn.
Training needs to have a more demonstrable impact in those areas."

Is it possible to make training demonstrably more effective while
halving your training expenditures? "Yes, we believe it is," Brennan
responds. "We'll make it happen in stages. We've already pulled virtually all the learning functions, including customer education, together
into our Global Learning organization. We did that to rationalize and
improve those processes and leverage the investment. Now we can
start to outsource more of it. We've also created the NCR University to
provide both learning and knowledge management and to facilitate
distance learning via the Internet and other alternative training
media. We'll end up with a learning structure that can flex. The technology industry is volatile. It wouldn't be kind to a rigid infrastructure.

"Of course, we can't hope to do all that while confining ourselves to
traditional methods," Brennan adds. "That's why we put out the RFP.
We're prepared to make radical changes in how we promote and man-

age learning in our corporation. We think such changes are appropriate for our industry in general and for our corporation, in particular."

For simplicity's sake, we structured this discussion around three options—make a strategic investment in reinventing T&D, selectively outsource T&D, or form an Insourcing Alliance. In reality, a spectrum of options is now emerging along this continuum. The ongoing demands on training to organize and work in innovative ways will surely expand the spectrum of options in the years ahead.

Two essentials in weighing your options for transforming your training organization, then, are keeping a close watch on the successful innovations now unfolding in T&D and being prepared to experiment with some innovations of your own.

Making the Business Case for Transformation

Most training people get considerable satisfaction from the mere fact that learning is taking place. We can certainly understand this. Learning can be inspiring, even thrilling. For most business leaders, however, learning must soon lead to making money, or the thrill is gone.

"I think training professionals let themselves and their work down when they don't focus on the business case for what they do," ventures Oracle's Mike Spurling. "It's great to have high ideals and to point to all these wondrous possibilities. But you still have to put together the case that addresses, Why would you invest in this *now*? and, What should we expect to get back? Without that analysis, it's just a lot of words. To fulfill its potential, training needs to get very, very crunchy."

Making the business case generally entails three steps:

1. Construct an economic rationale for change.

2. Work with your customers and other key stakeholders to improve your case.

3. Win explicit support for decisive action.

We've found that it's best to open your case by talking about opportunities to improve T&D's operating efficiency. As we show business leaders how they could get much more training for the same cost or even a lesser investment in the short term, we often underplay, to some extent, training's potential to change the organization over the long term. Why? When it comes to pondering the power of training, many executives are like sleeping giants. They've given the possibilities little serious thought, and they may not appreciate your disturbing their slumber with a lot of excited talk about training as a transformational force.

In contrast, most executives are immediately receptive to ideas for increasing returns on their investments. They live and breathe costs, profits, efficiency, and effectiveness. So we speak their language. We start by selling what they're buying.

The good news is that, armed with your business assessment of training, you're equipped to meaningfully discuss the economics of training with executives. You command all the data you need to get "crunchy" with senior managers about annual training costs per person, the cost of managing suppliers, investment comparisons against benchmarks, and the like.

Once you get executives talking about the economics of their training investment, they may quickly awaken to training's larger promise. Then *they* will raise the conversations to a higher plane—from short-term issues of cost and efficiency to the larger goal of enhancing training's effectiveness and long-term business value.

"Our company was cutting costs left and right," recalls Moore's Denny McGurer. "Every few months, my phone would ring and someone would tell me, 'You have to take some dollars out of your budget.' That was the atmosphere here when we conducted our business assessment of T&D. We did it without a lot of fanfare, and once I had the findings, I put them on the corner of my desk and waited for that next budget-cutting call to come," he says. "When it did, I said, 'Give me three months. I'll come back to you with a plan that will get you that same reduction in budget, but we'll get it by shifting to a very different concept of T&D.' They *had* to say yes," McGurer explains, "because I was responding to their cost-cutting request while, at the same time, doing exactly what we were all supposed to do—look for better ways to run the business."

Assessment findings in hand, McGurer set out to engage Moore's senior managers in a dialogue. "I spent a lot of time talking to the top eight or nine executives here, most of all with our CFO. We had some very focused one-on-one discussions. Historically, we hadn't had many opportunities for such intensive talks with such high-level peo-ple," he notes.

At first, the main topic was waste and how to get rid of it. "Our assessment had confirmed and quantified that there were very sub-stantial inefficiencies in our training investment," McGurer says. "But instead of jumping straight to the old 'slash and burn' strategy, we got into some good business discussions about fixed vs. variable costs, about how we might bring more discipline to our training opera-tions, and about how we could more consistently connect training to our business goals. Before you know it," he says, "the conversations had expanded from How do we cut the training budget? to What are our opportunities to significantly increase the business impact of T&D? Cost-efficiency is still a major part of our business plan for T&D," McGurer stresses, "but it took no time at all for our execs to widen their focus from that lone objective to the higher cause."

The business case you build and carry to key stakeholders may take shape as a paper document, a presentation, or even a relatively simple set of goals and operating principles. The key is to ensure that it looks and works like a business case that might come from any other part of the business.

If your customers are used to reviewing formal business case doc-uments, then you should prepare one for them. If they follow infor-mal processes to consider and sign off on major project work, then map the informal process and go that route. We usually research how line managers in the business made successful cases for, say, purchas-ing major technology or reorganizing a division, and then we model the business case for Running Training Like a Business accordingly.

Regardless of the format of your case, its main tasks are to propose the transformation, detail the required investment, credibly project the expected return on investment, and offer a blueprint for change.

Here, briefly described, are the main elements of business cases we've seen succeed.

Background

Briefly recap the methodology and key findings of the assessment, illustrating them with appropriate data.

Recommendations

Restate the specific recommendations for which you are now gathering support and commitment. Briefly describe the driving forces for change and the strategic rationale behind transforming training from a traditional function to an operation that works, in essence, as a business within the business.

Investment and Projected Return on Investment

State, in simple numerical terms, the total investment required to act on your recommendations. Couple the investment estimate with an equally direct and specific statement of the economic return the business should anticipate from the investment.

The following chart presents an example of how we would customarily present Investment and Projected Return on Investment in a business case.

	1999	2000	2001	2002	2003	Total
Total investment required to execute transformation (in thousands)	$442	$3,678	$ 2,200	$ 96	$ 96	$ 6,512
Potential savings to be delivered (estimated)	0	$4,375	$10,430	$10,430	$10,430	$35,665
Net per annum	–$442	$ 697	$ 8,230	$10,334	$10,334	$29,153

We also break out these numbers in terms of projected costs and return for each recommendation offered—operational savings, staff savings, external spending reductions, and so on.

How does one arrive at such projections? You first need a clear, credible, and quantified estimate of the business's current training costs. Since your business assessment has produced such an estimate, you need only apply factors for the clearly attainable benefits of unit cost reduction, buying aggregation, process efficiency, shifting from fixed costs to variable expenses, more businesslike personnel management practices, and the like. You can also present case histories documenting that comparable returns were, in fact, gained in other businesses in which training runs like a business.

In truth, showing that the cost of transition can be funded from savings in training costs—over a projectable, and not terribly long, period of time—describes but a fraction of the actual business benefits to be gained. Specifically, it describes the immediately quantifiable improvements in *efficiency,* all but ignoring the far greater potential business benefits that may be gained from increased training *effectiveness.* For reasons we've already stated, though, we like to begin by showing business leaders that they could get much more training for the same or a lesser investment. That is usually more than enough to gain their interest and initial support.

Financial Benefit Breakdown
We often follow our financial projections with a very brief narrative specifying how the estimated return on investment was calculated (and with what data), where the projected cost savings would be budgeted, and who would be accountable for delivering the projected cost savings.

Risk Analysis
Experienced business leaders know that it is prudent to look at the proverbial downside of any major project. So it's generally a good idea to take the lead in articulating the risks associated with the transition to Running Training Like a Business.

You can structure your risk analysis using a relatively simple matrix documenting the potential risks you or others perceive. You may also want to categorize each risk by its probability of occurrence (High/Medium/Low) and estimate the impact an occurrence would have on your projected economic benefits. Figure 6-4 presents a sample Risk Analysis matrix.

Proactively raising risks in this fashion offers three important advantages. One, it demonstrates that there's nothing Pollyannish about your thinking. Two, it provides a framework in which you can constructively invite others to talk about the risks they perceive.

Figure 6-4: Risk Analysis Matrix

Risks of Proceeding	Business (B) Risk or Project (P) Risk?	Probability High/Medium/Low	Impact on Projected Benefits	Mitigating Action	Action Team
Businesses do not buy into • Transitional recommendations • New T&D structure	P&B	Low Significant buy-in already attained	40% to 80%	Develop and implement ongoing communications plan – target region execs and heads of HR	Jones, Williams, and the transition team
Takeover/acquisition/merger of XYZ Corp. • At any stage beyond quarter 2 of 2000, XYZ Corp. will have invested considerable sums • Any new owners may have their own T&D organization and not wish to continue the project	P&B	High XYZ Corp. is often mentioned as a takeover target	Up to 100%	Follow XYZ Corp. policy – don't plan to go, plan to *grow* (i.e., act on assumption XYZ will remain a free-standing enterprise)	Board, Jones, and Williams
Loss of key personnel (e.g., project sponsor/GM of new T&D organization)	P	Low	10% to 20%	Develop succession plan to cover such contingencies	Williams
Technological obstacles to implementation of new T&D operating systems	P	Medium	25% to 50%	Form joint technology team with IT (see Appendix F)	Williams and Jacobs

Three, it articulates a risk management action plan, with account-abilities, for each risk identified. In sum, this form of risk analysis brings a measure of order and control to even the most horrific worst-case scenarios some business people tend to anticipate.

Chart a Course for the Dialogue

Once you've put together a draft of your business case for Running Training Like a Business, you're ready to share it with executives and other key stakeholders. Your ultimate goal, of course, is to win support for the case. But we'd urge you to focus first on an interim goal:

Try to make executives your *partners* in shaping your business case. See if they will work with you to enhance and refine it.

You'll increase the chances of that happening if you anticipate and chart the course of each dialogue. One should always enter executive-level discussions with a clear picture of how the conversation should unfold and of what must be done, each step of the way, to sustain the dialogue's momentum. Why? Most executives are notoriously purposeful by nature. They have little patience for meandering. If you fail to keep the process moving and on track, they will surely tire of it. That's not to suggest, though, that you should try to rush the process. You can't. Your customers and other process partners will set the pace, while you set the course.

The most productive business case deliberations tend to follow a consistent progression, starting with exploration of the opportunities to make the training investment more cost-effective. You may find, as we have, that certain aspects of these discussions consistently interest executives:

- Shifting from fixed cost to variable cost

- Unit cost reduction

- Buying aggregation

- System and process efficiency

- Staff/head count management

As your discussions about the efficiency of training progress, stay alert for chances to bridge into broader issues of training *effectiveness*, especially:

- Strategic linkage of training to business issues

- Increased access to a broad array of training

- Demonstrated value of the investment—moving the needle on the objectives the customer is paying you to help him or her achieve

When you raise this sort of issue with executives, you often make them, in effect, consultants to training. They draw on their long-term business management experience to suggest strategies and approaches T&D might apply to become more successful, in hard business terms.

Some of the most meaningful planning discussions we've had with executives, for example, were conducted over a chart we affectionately call the Camel Diagram.

Affection for a *diagram?* Sure, because more than most any kind of data we typically gather and present, the Camel Diagram projects training directly into the heart of executives'perceptions of value. As illustrated in Figure 6-5, the vertical axis of the Camel Diagram represents value added as defined by executives, while the horizontal axis represents the T&D supply chain. Ideally, the wavy line tracking executive-defined value and the vertical bars, representing how T&D devotes its resources and spends its budget, would be in sync. But they seldom are.

We were once working in a corporation where *value added* was officially defined as things customers are willing to pay for. So we made that concept of value the vertical axis of the Camel Diagram. The horizontal axis, as always, represented the supply chain of training activities.

To fill in the diagram, we took this two-axis diagram out and asked line managers—the people who were responsible for raising the revenues that paid for T&D—to rate each training activity in terms of value add. That is, Would your customers *pay* for this? The averages of their responses were plotted as the wavy black line. Then we looked at where the current training function devoted its resources and spent its budget. That data was illustrated with the vertical bars.

As is often the case, T&D's priorities were far from a perfect match to the camel-hump plot of what executives considered value-adding activity. We now had a very clear value-based picture of the current state of T&D. It was time to put the Camel Diagram to work. We looped back to the executives to share our findings and invited them to help us probe for the deeper meanings behind the findings.

Most of the executives we saw were immediately intrigued by the data. And why not? Finally, they were seeing something solid about

Figure 6-5: The Camel Diagram

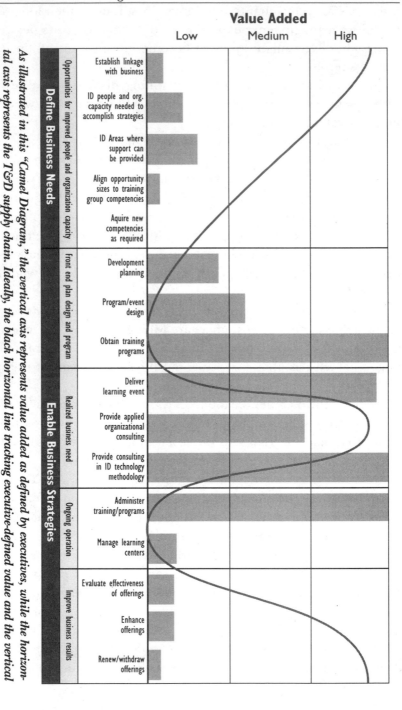

As illustrated in this "Camel Diagram," the vertical axis represents value added as defined by executives, while the horizontal axis represents the T&D supply chain. Ideally, the black horizontal line tracking executive-defined value and the vertical bars, representing how T&D devotes its resources and spends its budget, would be in sync. But they seldom are.

the business value of training! They jumped right in with reactions and advice.

"Clearly, what you want to do is look at all this low value-add stuff first, figure out which resources are focused on those elements of your supply chain, and redeploy them into higher value-adding work," said one tough and previously distant executive, clutching and intently studying the Camel Diagram. "But be careful. Some activities that are not 'value adding' are still important." How's that? we wondered.

"There are all kinds of important things customers won't pay for," he said. "You know, we need a new payroll system. Everyone has to pay their people, right? It's going to cost us something like ten million dollars. You think we can go out and say to customers: 'We're going to increase our prices so we can pay for that?' No way. It's not their problem. They don't want to pay for it. But we're still going to do it. It's the same for you. There are things you've got to do, no matter what we say."

Our point isn't that we could not interpret the data. We could. But there are a lot of different ways to view and then act on any given data set. We chose to develop our viewpoint *with* training's customers, and we used that shared viewpoint and those shared priorities to significantly improve our business case for transforming T&D into a train-ing enterprise. Our customers therefore understood our business rationale as well—and in some regards, better—than we did.

Match the Data to the Topic

Your success in starting and then sustaining your business planning dialogue will largely depend on how thoughtful you are in using your assessment data. It's not that you want to keep some data a secret. You've already reported the findings. Now, you and your key stake-holders will probe those findings, a segment at a time, to find their deeper meaning and build support for decisive actions.

So be selective. Choose a topic for discussion and present assess-ment data that relates directly to that particular emphasis—for exam-ple, "training process efficiency," "strategic linkage," or "demonstrat-ing business value." Share a few of the assessment findings that you believe are most indicative of your current situation around that issue. Briefly summarize what you see as the significance of what the assessment found. Then ask the executive to share his or her reactions. Ask open questions such as Do the assessment findings match your perceptions, or Do these findings surprise you? What would you suppose are the root causes of what we've found? Have you ever encountered comparable circumstances in other kinds of business operations? What did you do about them?

Don't be surprised or upset, by the way, if executives ask you for more data than you offer them initially. For example, if you demonstrate that your training processes are somewhat less efficient, on the whole, than are those of certain benchmarks, you may be asked if efficiency levels are uniform across all regions of the company, or if some regions actually excel while others drag down the average. When executives ask for additional data, it's a good sign. It means you're talking about something that matters to them.

Seek Out "Hard Cases" Early

You might be tempted to sidestep the "hard cases" among the ranks of your customers. But we suggest you seek out those individuals who are most likely to ask you tough questions and to challenge your logic early on. Talking with skeptics almost always brings out real potential weaknesses in your thinking that you would not otherwise discover until it's too late. Critics may also reveal great opportunities you had completely overlooked. By eliminating those weaknesses and acting on those opportunities, you ensure that the business case is truly worthy of everyone's support. What's more, you give yourself every chance to win over those who are least inclined to back your proposals.

At NatWest, the draft business plan was evaluated by more than 75 managers and executives over a period of almost 120 days. This process seemed painfully slow to us and to some of the team there. But we found that this intensive effort to gather input significantly strengthened the business case and our implementation plans.

As you proceed through the various discussion emphases we sketched out above, you and all those you engage in the dialogue will form a shared vision of a cost-effective, process-efficient training operation that offers all these strengths:

- Closely linked to the strategy of the business

- Driven by business objectives

- Capable of consistently delivering clearly perceived unmistakable business value

What's more, you'll have shared your recommendations for building just such a training organization and invited your customers to share their reactions, thoughts, and suggestions, which you then used to revise and improve your business case. Now you are ready to ask key stakeholders for their formal commitment to move ahead.

Conclusion

Once your business case is complete and accepted by your customers, you'll find you spend a lot less time explaining what training does and why. Nor will you be scrambling to justify training's existence with isolated, after-the-fact measurements. The customers you serve will know just what you're about, and just what to expect from training in the way of unmistakable value.

Keys to Weighing Your Options and Making the Business Case

➤ First, consider whether transforming T&D is warranted and feasible.

➤ Study innovations under way in T&D and actively consider options that range beyond what's tried and true in your organization.

➤ Base your case on economics.

➤ Focus first on cost and efficiency, then effectiveness.

➤ Follow established pathways to project approval.

➤ Chart a course for the dialogue.

➤ Structure interactions to make executives your partners.

➤ Match the data to the topic.

➤ Seek out contrary views early on.

➤ Refine your perceptions and improve your recommendations.

➤ Ask for formal commitments of support.

7

Planning: Design a Value Machine

◆◇

Now that you've conducted your assessment and made a compelling case for Running Training Like a Business, you may come under pressure to instantly launch a new training organization. ("It makes great sense, so let's go!") That sort of demand can be intoxicating. After all, you've worked hard to stir up just such enthusiasm. Our advice? Enjoy the feeling. But keep a clear head. Your next few moves will be crucial. Figure 7-1 lays out the key steps for this part of the transformation, the Planning phase.

"When you decide to build a house, you don't immediately pour concrete. First, you draw a blueprint," notes Mary Maloney, a Forum

Figure 7-1: Key Steps for Planning

PHASES

	ASSESSING	PLANNING	INSTALLING	RUNNING
KEY STEPS	Understand Business Issues, Strategies, and Organization	Scope Full-Scale Operations		
	Assess Training Offerings, Processes, People vs. Best Practices	Map and Structure Future Organization and Relationships		
	Identify Customer Expectations and Level of Satisfaction	Spec the Installation		
	Conduct Financial/ Vendor Analysis and Technology Assessment	Develop Employee Transition Plan		
	Develop Recommendations, Vision, and CSFs	Develop Organizational Communication Plan		

colleague who pioneered much of the planning process described in this chapter. "Even before you draw your blueprint," she says, "you ask questions like, Who will live here? How much space will they need? What's their lifestyle? Taking a little time to determine those things in advance is common sense. The same common sense applies in managing a major business project."

Transition

Mary speaks from our collective experience. For a while, we lumped the Planning and Installing phases together into a single phase we called Transition. In fact, the term *transition* remains very much a part of our working vernacular. It refers to the series of actions required to move from the current state of training to the desired state of Running Training Like a Business, once you've committed to that objective.

We've found, though, that this transition is best pursued via two distinct phases: Planning and Installing. This ensures that Planning, which must be thorough, isn't compromised by the sense of urgency you've raised for creating a new training organization. There are several key distinctions between Planning and Installing, including those laid out in the table below.

Planning Steps	Installing Steps
• Determine how many people are needed for the new organization	• Hire, align, and train staff
• Envision the product/ service offering	• Create catalog, registration, and tracking techniques
• Identify resource requirements	• Negotiate resource contracts
• Decide on performance priorities	• Create business scorecard
• Craft detailed project plan	• Track and report progress against plan

You enter into Planning, then, not as an isolated exercise, but as the first half of an overall transition project, which will continue on through the actual installation of the new training organization.

In this chapter, we'll first describe the overall transition project, giving special attention to the keys to forming a strong transition team and to getting your transition off to a good start. Then we'll itemize the critical questions the Planning half of your transition should answer. Finally, we'll walk through each of the five key steps in the Planning phase:

- Scope the full-scale operation

- Map and structure the organization and relationships

- Spec the installation

- Develop the employee transition plan

- Develop a communication plan

The Transition Project

The transition project is complex and ambitious. You will pursue many outcomes simultaneously. Here, as in the Assessing phase, we've found that it is best to start with those ends in mind.

Specifically, your transition project should yield a new training organization equipped with all the fundamentals of a high-performing business. That gives you a lot to think about, and even more to do, especially if your business is large.

The Dynamic Business Scorecard, introduced in Chapter 3 and discussed in Chapter 5, is a useful tool for tangibly defining all that must be done to transition from a traditional training organization to one that's prepared to run like a business. In Figure 7-2 we present the scorecard once again, this time filled in with deliverables.

The transition project requires a strong project leader, preferably someone with extensive experience managing large-scale projects that command significant resources and rely on high levels of cross-functional and inter-organizational action. The project leader's first task is forecasting how many hours of work and which tasks will actually have to get done to effect the transition. He or she can then develop a resource plan and assemble an appropriate transition team.

Figure 7-2: Transition Project Deliverables

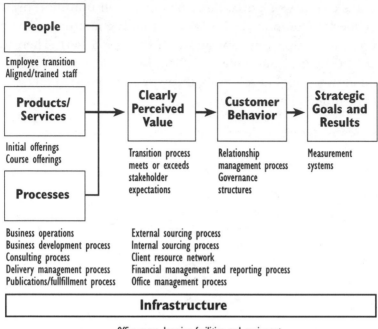

In the Appendix, we present a tool called the Scoping Questionnaire that can help Transition Project Leaders accurately forecast the length of the transition, define the size and capability requirements for the transition team, and accurately forecast the length of the transition. This tool may subsequently be used by the entire transition team to develop a clear understanding of current T&D capabilities, activities, and resources; to help define the size, shape, and mission of the new training organization; and to identify specific gaps between current resources and capabilities and those needed for a successful transition to Running Training Like a Business.

The transition team should include much more than just training expertise. Who's going to spec the financial systems? Who'll design the information management infrastructure? Who knows about publications management? Who's your expert in recruiting? Who can take on curriculum design? You want a team that has the breadth of experience required to shape a *business,* which is quite different from reorganizing a training department. Our advice to Transition Project Leaders is to go out and get the people you need, whether you have to borrow them, rent them, or hire them. If you've made the economic case for Running Training Like a Business, you've already justified the investment.

As you assemble your team, make sure everyone is up to speed on the assessment findings (that is, the current state of training) and that they grasp the business case (the rationale for transforming training). Explain that the transition team will first determine what's realistically required to effect that change, and *then* make it happen.

Pacing the Transition Project

Anytime you climb into the driver's seat of change, speed is a key concern. Drive too slow and you risk losing precious momentum. Drive too fast, and you can make key stakeholders anxious, which is a very bad idea, since you must have their active support all through the transition to Running Training Like a Business. Our approach? Drive hard, but watch to make sure everyone is still along for the ride.

If you're going too fast, you may notice some stakeholders asking for frequent rest stops. Perhaps they'll dredge up old concerns that you thought were resolved, or they may hesitate to sign off on a key action step for no clear reason. If this happens to you, remember that there may *be* no clear reason. Your stakeholders may simply be uncomfortable with the pace of change. In fact, you should probably expect that some people will experience anxiety of imprecise origins. Such feelings are quite natural in the midst of an organizational transformation. So slow down. Do what you must to help them get comfortable. Usually, all you need to do is take some time to sit down and talk things through. We've found that people often resolve their own apprehensions in the course of such talks, and you're then free to forge on.

When you're going too slow, you may notice your fellow travelers nodding off. That is, they'll lose their sense of excitement and anticipation about the transition. They arrive late for meetings, are slow to return your calls, and stop asking for the latest news on the transition. When you see these signs, press a bit harder on the accelerator. It's time to make things happen.

How long should your transition project take? Our answer, predictably, is: It depends. What's the scope of the new training organization you're planning to build? Is your business culture accustomed to change on this scale? Are there compelling business reasons to push the process through with extraordinary dispatch? Any timeline we suggest would have to take such situation-specific factors thoroughly into account. Nevertheless, the question merits a concrete answer. You do want to enter transition with a firm schedule because, with rare exceptions, business projects should not be open-ended. Transition projects in which we've participated have run from a minimum of 2 months to a maximum of 18 months, from the beginning of Planning through Installing the new training organization. The sample timeline in Figure 7-3 illustrates how a transition might unfold when the transition team works intensively and effectively.

Figure 7-3: Sample Timeline

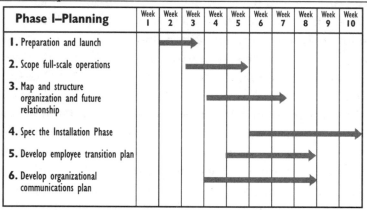

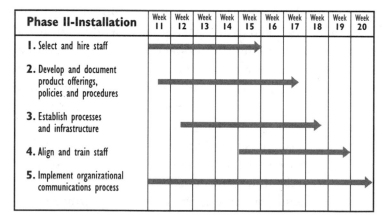

Critical Questions for Planning

Having used the Dynamic Business Scorecard to frame up the transition project deliverables, we often apply the same framework to identify the critical questions that should be answered during the Planning phase.

We've found that it is generally more enlightening to work *backward* through the scorecard as you define critical questions for Planning. As Figure 7-4 illustrates, at this stage we recommend that you focus first on the ends—what training should do, for whom, and to what effect—so those ends can in turn shape the means, which include the People, Products/Services, Processes, and Infrastructure of the new training enterprise.

Figure 7-4: Focusing First on Ends

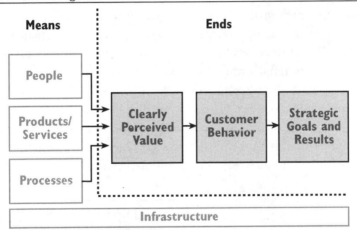

You can't design a training organization that delivers clearly perceived value without first defining, in detailed and concrete terms, what your customers are trying to accomplish, exploring how the new training organization can advance customers toward their business goals, and determining how your contributions can be credibly documented. Figure 7-5 outlines key questions you can use to define your strategic goals and results.

Planning should erase any and all ambiguity about who your new training organization will serve and what those customers truly value. See Figure 7-6 for questions to help you define the value you will

Figure 7-5: Results Questions

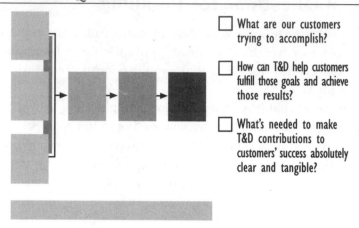

☐ What are our customers trying to accomplish?

☐ How can T&D help customers fulfill those goals and achieve those results?

☐ What's needed to make T&D contributions to customers' success absolutely clear and tangible?

deliver, seek out champions and carefully consider how and when to involve customers in shaping your training enterprise.

The new training organization will be, in essence, a business unto itself. It will therefore have more (and more explicit) processes than does the traditional training function. Further, each of those processes must be made highly efficient and thoroughly reliable. Figure 7-7 lists sample questions for Process planning.

Some portion of what you currently offer will probably fit into the new value equation. But the only way to objectively assess *which* portion will be valuable is to wipe the slate clean. No course can be

Figure 7-6: Customer Value Questions

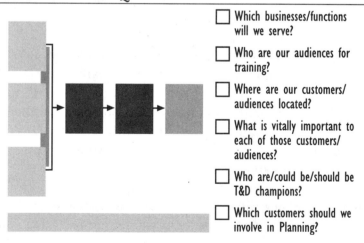

☐ Which businesses/functions will we serve?

☐ Who are our audiences for training?

☐ Where are our customers/ audiences located?

☐ What is vitally important to each of those customers/ audiences?

☐ Who are/could be/should be T&D champions?

☐ Which customers should we involve in Planning?

Figure 7-7: Process Questions

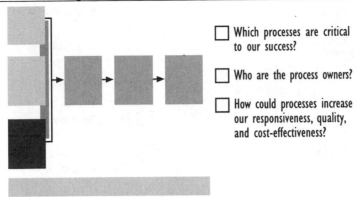

☐ Which processes are critical to our success?

☐ Who are the process owners?

☐ How could processes increase our responsiveness, quality, and cost-effectiveness?

sacred, no matter whose "baby" it might be. In fact, it's best not to think too much about what you already have, at least not at first. Planning should explore questions such as those in Figure 7-8, to help you envision a mix of training products and services ideally matched to customer needs. Let neither sentimentality nor pride of authorship compromise the new training organization's capacity to deliver value.

On the one hand, you must staff the new training organization with people who can deliver what customers demand; on the other, you must treat all employees with exemplary fairness and respect, whether or not they become part of the new training organization. That won't be easy, but this one you have to get right. Nothing is

Figure 7-8: Products/Services Questions

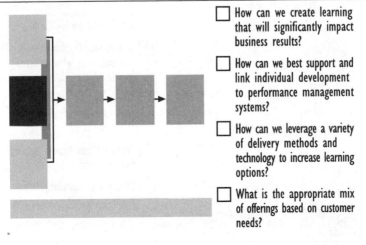

☐ How can we create learning that will significantly impact business results?

☐ How can we best support and link individual development to performance management systems?

☐ How can we leverage a variety of delivery methods and technology to increase learning options?

☐ What is the appropriate mix of offerings based on customer needs?

Figure 7-9: People Questions

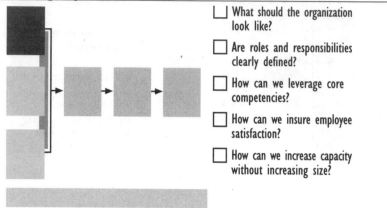

☐ What should the organization look like?

☐ Are roles and responsibilities clearly defined?

☐ How can we leverage core competencies?

☐ How can we insure employee satisfaction?

☐ How can we increase capacity without increasing size?

more crucial to the success of your transition and the reputation of your new training organization. Figure 7-9 suggests some People questions to ask during the Planning phase.

While content-driven training functions may not spend much time thinking about infrastructure issues, a customer-driven business must. You won't get far into the Planning phase before the realization hits you: Infrastructure links you to your customers. It can also make or break your efforts to reliably deliver effective and efficient training. See Figure 7-10 for Infrastructure questions that should be asked during Planning.

That completes our summary of critical questions to be answered during the Planning phase. Now let's explore what specific actions

Figure 7-10: Infrastructure Questions

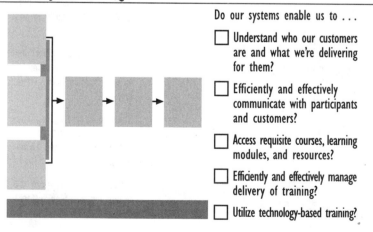

Do our systems enable us to . . .

☐ Understand who our customers are and what we're delivering for them?

☐ Efficiently and effectively communicate with participants and customers?

☐ Access requisite courses, learning modules, and resources?

☐ Efficiently and effectively manage delivery of training?

☐ Utilize technology-based training?

your transition team must take to develop sound answers to these and other questions.

Scope Full-Scale Operations

What missions should the new training organization take on? That, in essence, is what scoping your full-scale operations is all about. This is when you carve out a clear role for the new training organization, one that enables you to contribute maximum business value with maximum efficiency.

"We've found that one key to delivering consistent value is not trying to be all things to all people. You need to focus on areas where you can make the greatest impact," says Gene Cox, a trainer and consultant in one of our learning alliances. "For example, you might decide that safety, quality, and product training could be best addressed within your various operating divisions. That's fine. Let it be."

"We've put a lot of emphasis on sales skills, on leadership and management skills, on presentation skills, and on a host of similar areas," says Allen Roberts of Mellon's The Learning Investment. "We're focused on things that we've found can help the bank raise revenue and drive the bottom line."

"One of our planning objectives was to outsource all of the transactional work—the 'repetitive tasks,' if you will," reports Madeline Fassler of Kaiser Permanente. "We decided to get that work out of our office, so we could spend our time focusing on more strategic types of value-adding activity."

The great power of data-driven planning is that it lets you make hard choices that are strategically sound and thoroughly defensible from a business standpoint. Your new training organization's mission won't be based on anyone's intuition. Rather, you'll scope the new training operation based on assessment findings, on best practices benchmarks, on what the businesses you serve say they need, and on what you must have to run training like a business.

You can expect that, once everyone sees for sure that a big change is coming, some people will start to ring a fence around their current responsibilities or facilities and say, "This isn't part of whatever it is you're planning." Such territoriality is part of human nature. Data is

how you rise above territoriality and other emotion-charged positions. It is the key to shaping a training organization that is justifiable
and right from a business perspective, period.

We've found, in fact, that it is generally wise to continue active
data gathering during the Planning phase, although your data needs
have changed. Now you're getting down to real nuts and bolts comparisons between the current state of training versus what you need
to build. It's time to determine the details: Exactly how many people
do we have, where are they, and what can they do? How close is the
current registration system to the one we'll need? Do we have software for project management? Is there a Human Resources
Information System we can interface with? There's so much you still
need to know to determine, concretely, what will be entailed in making the transition from the current state. The Scoping Questionnaire
presented in the Appendix should give you a good sense of the range
of data most transition teams require to effectively plan.

The tools you choose for scoping should enable you to get down
to comparable levels of detail across a similarly wide spectrum of
transition issues. There are many, many decisions to make; you want
to command all the data and perspectives you need to choose your
focus and leverage your resources wisely.

Your choice of what training services to offer will be among the most
consequential outcomes of the scoping process. True, the offering decisions you make in the Planning phase can be—in fact, *must* be—modi-
fied as your new training organization gains experience. But your orig-
inal choices are crucial. If your initial offerings are poorly matched to
your customers' needs, you may never have the chance to evolve.

"It's very easy to conceive your training offerings at a superficial
level, but if you want to put a meaningful plan together, you can't just
say, 'We'll do some of this and a bit of that.' That's not the way a business works," Forum's Mary Maloney cautions. "So many other
Planning decisions hinge on your offerings, you really need to generate detailed forecasts, based on projected demand, that specify just
how much of what you'll actually deliver, as well as *how* you're going
to deliver it. If you don't have that part nailed down, how are you
going to structure your new organization, figure out how to staff it,
identify key suppliers, and all the rest?"

Map and Structure the Future Organization and Relationships

As scoping brings your new training organization's mission into focus, your transition team can start to explore questions like these: What should the new training organization look like? How should it operate?

You won't have to start from scratch. By this time, you'll have arrived at some sound presumptions about what kind of training organization you should build.

"I envisioned a very business-focused operation that looks, feels, and acts like a business," recalls Moore's Denny McGurer. "There was definitely a sketch in our minds of what it would be, even before we actually started to map and structure the new training alliance."

The typical business is led by executives and line managers. Training that's run like a business has a General Manager, plus managers in charge of customer-contact functions and all the internal operations. If the new training organization is large, it may even have multiple staff functions, such as Marketing and Communications, Finance, Human Resources, and Information Technology. The transition team develops detailed job descriptions for all the various positions, as shown in the table below.

Position	Primary Responsibilities
Manager of Relationship Managers and Consultants	• Lead, manage, and develop the Relationship Management and Consultant team and processes • Ensure the identification and development of best solutions to meet business needs and produce business results • Maintain strong relationships with senior managers in client organizations
Business/Delivery Operations Manager	• Lead, manage, and develop the business operations team and processes, including delivery management, financial management, technology, publications/fulfillment, internal/external sourcing, and office administration

- Take responsibility for quality of internal operations, management of costs, invoicing, and client satisfaction
- Lead and manage the delivery operations team and processes to ensure flawless delivery to the client organization
- Provide direction on policies, processes, and procedures for all aspects of the operation, including registration, facilities scheduling, materials production and fulfillment, and vendor coordination

Customer Service Representative (CSR)
- Coordinate all logistical aspects of program delivery, including participant registration and confirmation, facilities scheduling, materials production and fulfillment, instructor communication, and project/course finances
- Manage relationships with client site coordinators for setup of site facilities and management of feedback and client communications

Desktop Publisher/ Production
- Publish high-quality presentation and training programs
- Manage external desktop publishers and practices
- Manage publications and fulfillment process

Administrator Coordinator
- Provide administrative support; coordinate and manage office activities
- Respond to customers and coach or counsel participants about offerings by phone
- Prepare presentations using desktop publishing software

Your new training organization will be considerably more complex than the traditional training function. It must encompass all the core processes and roles one finds in any business. Chances are your organizational chart will look much like those found in most businesses.

You may find, though, that a traditional organizational chart is a bit too flat to capture the essence of Running Training Like a Business. We prefer a concept that focuses on interactions that will generate clearly perceived value for customers. For while it is important to diagram a management hierarchy for the new training organization, the vision of what your training organization will look like and of how it will work truly emerges when you picture it from the customer's perspective.

The customer-focused organizational chart, as shown in Figure 7-11, begins with the front lines, where we find Relationship Managers (RMs) and Customer Service Representatives (CSRs) teaming directly with customers to understand business issues, identify corresponding training needs, and manage the overall business relationship.

The new training organization's Consultants join in the customer-contact loop on an as-needed basis, while also working with resources internal to the training organization to design, develop, and deliver training solutions and provide variable-cost services to customers.

The various business functions within the training enterprise

Figure 7-11: Customer-focused Organizational Chart

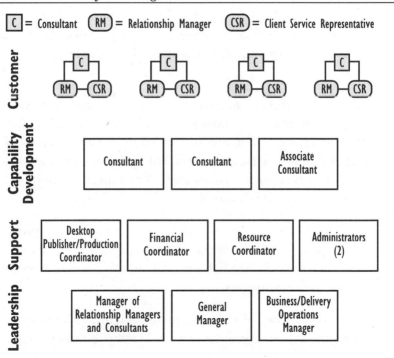

develop products and services, ensure efficient and timely delivery, manage the finances of the operation, and handle administrative duties. Standing behind and working for the entire operation are the General Manager and main line managers, whose collective duties include making major business decisions, providing leadership, managing and developing people, keeping the training organization close to its customers, and continuously improving its overall capabilities.

The managers of the newly forming T&D enterprise need not take on all those responsibilities themselves. Planning should seriously consider creating an advisory board to work with the new training organization's managers. Specifically, we've found such boards an excellent mechanism for keeping a training organization attuned to the larger business conditions, needs, and priorities of its customers. Advisory boards can also provide timely, ongoing feedback and serve as champions of learning. They often prove excellent partners, too, for shaping new systems to measure training's business value.

Here are a few important lessons we've learned about forming and working with advisory boards:

- Start advisory boards as early on as you can—during Planning, if possible. It's harder to start boards once the new training organization has been in operation for a while.

- Consider forming two different boards—a strategic advisory board of senior management customers as well as a middle-management advisory board to address more tactical and unit-specific questions. This helps ensure that each board considers issues that all members will find appropriate and relevant.

- Charter these advisory groups to help you shape learning strategies. (Oversight of the daily operations of the training enterprise should belong solely to the training organization's own managers.)

- Run advisory board meetings professionally, with pre-set agendas, formal presentations, and facilitated discussions.

- Don't assume all board members will fully understand the promise of training. Make presentations that highlight training's power to help them—in immediately relevant and tangible ways—a regular agenda item.

- Enroll board members to become evangelists for the training enterprise.

Mellon, for example, has initiated a Training Leadership Council, composed of senior training managers from across Mellon's diverse groups of businesses. The council convenes regularly to discuss business issues and training's role in providing solutions. Mellon is also forming an advisory board made up of senior business leaders, whose charter will cover issues that go beyond individual business lines to provide a corporationwide perspective on training.

Last, but far from least, your map of the new training organization should include a detailed picture of the infrastructure required to support your new training organization. Infrastructure planning addresses facilities and equipment needs, supply chain issues, and a host of other practical considerations. However, we often pay special attention to how information will be managed for optimum business performance. You may be surprised by just how much information must flow, quickly and reliably, through a training organization that runs like a business. This element of infrastructure planning alone can be a formidable project, one that should be tackled by a task team with IT expertise.

"Be honest with yourself about the challenges you're taking on," advises Forum's Ellen Foley, an experienced transition leader. "Ask yourself, What might be a show-stopper? In a lot of places, we've found that information technology is a big obstacle. Often, you can't run the new training organization on the available systems. So we routinely ask IT to get involved with our transition teams very early on. We can't go forward without them."

Plan With the Future in Sight

A common mistake in business planning is assuming that the future will look much like the present. Such an assumption could prove especially harmful to your plans for Running Training Like a Business, as most signs point to enormous and imminent change in the training environment.

The twin engines driving change are demands for training that is immediate, relevant, and accessible, coupled with ongoing breakthroughs in the technology available to deliver such training. As illustrated in Figure 7-12, corporate classrooms may soon be like ocean liners in the jet age—a luxury, not a necessity.

Spec the Installation

As the vision of your new training enterprise is taking shape, your transition team can begin specifying how and when you will put the new organization in place.

Detailed action planning is essential. If you simply send a lot of people off on different streams of activity in the hope that their work will somehow all fit together down the line, it probably won't.

This need for coordination and careful sequencing of work plays out in dozens of ways, all through the Planning phase as well as the installation itself. Your decisions on what training services to offer are very closely connected, for example, to your presumptions about your sources of income and your decisions about budget, which in turn shape your financial systems, your pricing strategies, and so forth.

"When a transition team is at its best, it performs like a fine orchestra," says our colleague Mary Maloney. "A very diverse mix of talent, expertise, and experience works as one to produce something none of them could produce on their own."

Work on a Budget

Of course, even a fine orchestra works on a budget. At the beginning of each transition project, we typically develop a budget that makes realistic and whole projections of the actual costs to be incurred (and by whom) in effecting the transition.

Figure 7-12: Planning with the Future in Sight

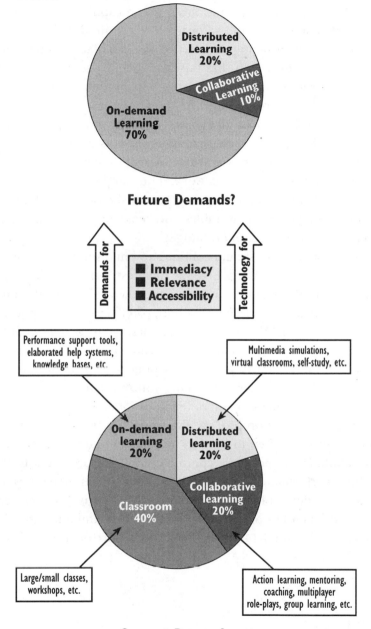

Future Demands?

Current Demands

The largest component of the transition project budget is usually the cost of people. In many instances, some capital investment (for office space, computers, and so on) is also required. Since the costs for Planning and Installing are part of the calculations included in the business case—which has already been presented to, and approved by, significant stakeholders—you probably won't need to justify your budget further.

But the transition team does have an obligation to work within that budget. In fact, we view that obligation as an opportunity to demonstrate that training is moving toward a more disciplined and businesslike approach to all its work. The sample memorandum in Figure 7-13 illustrates how transition teams should track their costs against specific project deliverables and make adjustments, as needed, to bring their project in on budget.

"The transition work should continue to build support for the concept of Running Training Like a Business," notes Ellen Foley. "Technically, you've made your case, and now you're into the implementation. But all through the transition, you'll have lots of opportunities to further engage the remaining skeptics. We try to recruit at least some skeptics onto the transition team, because you can often win them over by involving them. In general, it's important to realize that you must go on proving yourself and selling yourself to all your customers. That never stops, really, just as it never stops for any business."

Early in the transition process, the transition team at Moore conducted an initial survey to identify key stakeholders' expectations. Team members subsequently conducted follow-up surveys to measure their performance against those expectations. They reported the survey findings biweekly throughout the transition period, to demonstrate their customer focus and their determination to deliver on promises. Figure 7-14 shows a sample report of those performance ratings.

Figure 7-13: Sample Budget Memo

Memorandum

To   Project Leaders

From Project Manager

Date November 4, 1998

Re   Transition Budget Update

Please find the updated budget projections for the transition on the attached spreadsheet. If our estimates hold through the final phase of the project, we should come in within projected ranges.

Here is the current budget status for the five deliverables that are still in progress*:

Deliverable	% Over/Under Budget	$ Amount
D1	10%	$1,896
D3	−28%	−$2,280
D5	3%	$ 690
D7	9%	$2,505
D8	−23%	−$3,690

D8 D8 team forecasts needing $2,000 to complete work. D8 deliverable will therefore be completed under budget by 18–23 percent. (Thanks, D8. That sure helps the rest of us!)

D3 D3 leader, we need to factor in the software purchases we discussed yesterday. When you get that pricing, please send me a revised status. (It would be ideal if the added software costs could be covered by your surplus. Possible?)

D7 Just under half of the D7 deliverable cost is related to Project Leader time. Last week, you estimated that 11 additional hours of PL time is needed. Please confirm that this will suffice, or provide updated estimate of PL time/cost. Thanks.

D1 Ten percent is manageable, but if you anticipate it could go higher, let's talk. I have a few ideas that might help.

* If any numbers in the table don't match the latest budget status figure you
  provided, please alert me before we get together on Tuesday.

Figure 7-14: Expectations Survey

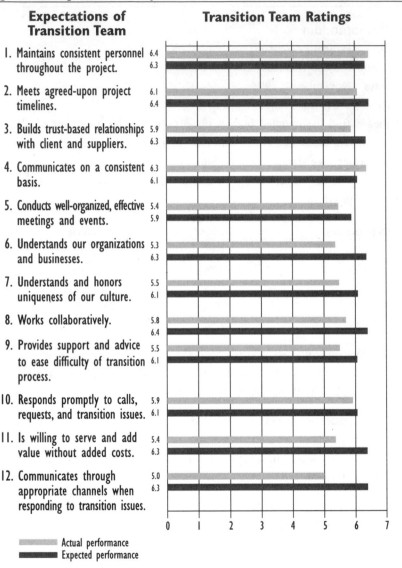

Expectations of Transition Team

Transition Team Ratings

1. Maintains consistent personnel throughout the project. 6.4 6.3

2. Meets agreed-upon project timelines. 6.1 6.4

3. Builds trust-based relationships with client and suppliers. 5.9 6.3

4. Communicates on a consistent basis. 6.3 6.1

5. Conducts well-organized, effective meetings and events. 5.4 5.9

6. Understands our organizations and businesses. 5.3 6.3

7. Understands and honors uniqueness of our culture. 5.5 6.1

8. Works collaboratively. 5.8 6.4

9. Provides support and advice to ease difficulty of transition process. 5.5 6.1

10. Responds promptly to calls, requests, and transition issues. 5.9 6.1

11. Is willing to serve and add value without added costs. 5.4 6.3

12. Communicates through appropriate channels when responding to transition issues. 5.0 6.3

0 1 2 3 4 5 6 7

Actual performance
Expected performance

Develop the Employee Transition Plan

A bit earlier, we suggested that nothing is more crucial to the success of your transition than how you select and treat people. Developing an employee transition plan is therefore among the most sensitive and consequential challenges facing your transition team.

You *must* recruit the best talent available. Specifically, training that runs like a business needs people with these qualifications:

- Are interested in and have the appropriate skills for the job position

- Demonstrate customer focus

- Understand business

- Demonstrate the capacity and willingness to be versatile in supporting an evolving team

The cold reality is that some members of your current training staff may not meet those criteria.

We've often found the Relationship Manager (sometimes called Business Liaison) position especially difficult to fill from within the existing T&D staff. Once or twice we've placed people in these positions we shouldn't have. Every position in the new organization is vital. You have to stick to your guns: Only someone with the requisite experience and qualifications should get the job.

At the same time, you must treat everyone with respect and dignity. "We worked especially hard to make sure there were no 'losers' in this transition. If we didn't do that—if we callously cut loose 30 percent of our former T&D staff—they'd say we didn't take care of those people, and our new training alliance would be hampered by the lingering hostility," says Moore's Denny McGurer. "We made sure that everyone who didn't join the new training alliance transitioned into something that made them happy."

Employees who've experienced the transition say one key to treating them right is empathy. The transition process has to respect and respond to their very natural hopes, fears, and concerns.

"The company I worked for had a history of taking people like me—an engineer—and assigning them to a training role," says Gene Cox. "We'd do a lot of self-study, learn from our mistakes, and kind of stumble along until we became more proficient. In fact, quite a few who followed that track became much better than proficient. But with the new training organization coming in, the bar was suddenly raised. Our training group was being replaced with a business-driven, world-class training operation. We had the chance to be part of it, *if* we were good enough. I guess all of us wondered, Are we?"

Intriguingly, we can't recall anyone in the training functions we've helped transform asking for anything like a guarantee. "The notion that it's natural for people to resist change is just plain wrong," Cox insists. "People often like change. They can accept and be excited by a measure of uncertainty, too. What they resist is the idea that you can drive change right over them, without considering their concerns and their need to be successful. All any of us wanted, I think, was a fair chance to go on being successful, in one capacity or another. And each of us got that."

In every training alliance we've created to date, some members of the former training staff wound up joining the new training organization. Those who did not join the training enterprise transitioned to new positions inside their company or chose to leave to pursue other opportunities. Not only did these individuals get the chance to go on being successful, they've also made good on that chance with remarkable consistency.

Your employee transition plan should spell out—in specific and concrete terms—precisely how you will evaluate, select, and communicate with all employees. It should also articulate the processes you'll use for managing the employee transition and orientation. These are some of the key steps in developing the employee transition plan:

- Review the projected structure and develop a corresponding staffing strategy.

- Finalize a list of available positions and position descriptions.

- Establish a liaison with the HR Manager.

- Select an interview team.

- Define selection criteria.

- Articulate the interview and selection process.

- Design an employee transition communication plan.

- Design an orientation and on-boarding process.

Figure 7-15 presents an example of how one transition team articulated its interview and selection process.

The bottom line on planning your employee transition? Recognize that you are, in many regards, walking into a potential minefield. There are more risks than you can possibly anticipate. Yet this is ground you must cross to run training like a business.

Figure 7-15: Interview and Selection Process Map

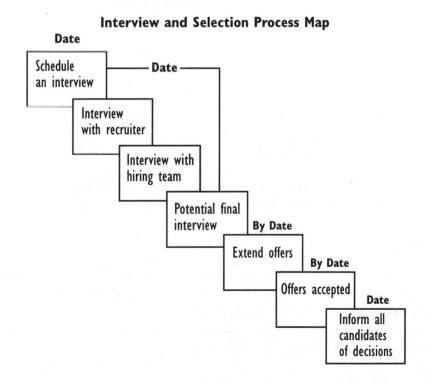

Fortunately, careful planning, coupled with absolute honesty and a genuine commitment to ensuring that no one gets hurt by the transformation, will enable your new training organization to traverse even this hazardous terrain, and come out on the other side better for the experience.

Develop the Organizational Communication Plan

Typically a subgroup of transition team members works in a task force with several key customer stakeholders to develop the overall communications strategy and plans, which should carry through the start-up of the new training organization. Here are steps you'll likely want to include in your communications planning:

1. Review why the new training organization is being formed, who was instrumental in that decision, the emerging goals and success measures for training, and the transition process and timeline.

2. Identify the audiences for communications.

3. Develop overall guiding principles for communications.

4. Identify communications options and asterisk those that are preferred (already in use and credible within the company) modes of communications.

5. Determine which audiences should receive what kinds of communications, and with what frequency.

6. Develop measures of success.

Good communications planning always begins with a focus on the target audiences, which in this case include all your stakeholder groups. Good communications planning also takes nothing for granted. Make everything as explicit as possible, to ensure that some members of the planning group are not acting on a set of core presumptions that, down the line, turn out to be different from those guiding some others who are also shaping the plans.

Often, your ability to do these things well depends on the kinds of tools you use. Your communications planners can complete a simple stakeholder diagram, as illustrated in Figure 7-16, to specify your target audiences, grouping them according to their presumed information needs.

Figure 7-16: Sample Stakeholder Diagram

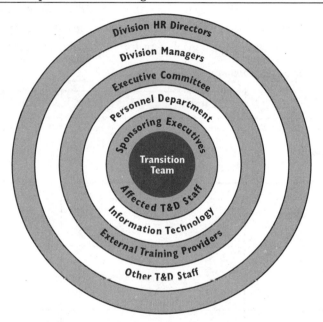

It is only reasonable to expect, after all, that fellow members of your transition team will have different information needs than would your senior executives. Similarly, external training providers will have somewhat different information needs than would internal training resources.

Audiences with whom you expect to work directly during the transition and installation, such as fellow members of the transition team, are placed in the center of the diagram. Those with whom you expect to have somewhat less frequent and direct contact, such as affected T&D staff and managers, are charted in the next circle. Those who are important to the success of the project, but with whom you and your team will have limited contact, belong in the outer circles. Examples of those who generally fit here include leaders of business units, HR, and senior executives. You proceed in this manner until you've charted all your key stakeholder audiences.

Having arrived at a shared picture of your target audiences, you can get down to deciding how to communicate with each through the crucial weeks ahead.

Again, a good tool can make quite a difference. The strategic communications framework shown in Figure 7-17, for example, can help organize your thinking as your group plots out the essential ingredients of communications strategy: goals, audience, media, and frequency.

Figure 7-17: Strategic Communications Framework

	Planning	Installing	Running
Goals			
Audience			
Media			
Frequency			

We'd add that you need not wait until all your plans are final to start communicating. It's critical, in fact, to communicate throughout the transition.

"My advice is to communicate to a factor of infinity," offers Ellen Foley. "Early and often, you want to remind the organization about the purpose of this work, where we are headed, and what's possible. You may have told them, but that doesn't mean it stays on their mind."

In sum, plan to communicate all through the transition. Convey a clear sense of progress: Let people know that you really are *getting* somewhere. If people don't hear anything, they tend to think nothing is happening. Your news doesn't have to be earth-shattering to be worth sharing. Communicating helps everyone feel comfortable with the changes as they unfold. And if they're comfortable, it's easier for them to support your efforts.

Conclusion

You can think of the Planning experience we've described in this chapter as a kind of sneak preview. This is how it will feel to be part of a training organization that runs like a business, because this planning process is businesslike in every sense of the word.

It rests squarely on a proven business case. Before you even begin to plan, you have the answers you'll need when someone inevitably asks, "*Why* are you doing this again?"

It is thoroughly results-driven. In fact, the whole planning process is an exercise in working backwards from a set of outcomes previously identified as beneficial and/or even crucial to the business as a whole.

This form of Planning is based on data and facts. It is carried out as a business project, disciplined by the same kinds of pre-set schedules, firm forecasts, and finite operating budgets that govern any other business project.

Most of all, this Planning process is a significant risk. It requires a sizable up-front investment in time, money, and other resources. So it's not the kind of project you can quit on halfway through without someone calling you on the carpet to ask you what went wrong. Of course, that's how it generally is in business. To make something big happen, you have to put a little skin in the game—*your* skin. Believe us, by the time you wrap up Planning, you'll have learned just how much you really like living with risk.

Keys to Successful Planning

➤ Take time to draw your blueprint.

➤ Start by identifying transition deliverables.

➤ Forecast actual work to be completed during the transition.

➤ Recruit needed experts onto transition team.

➤ Identify critical questions for the Planning phase.

➤ Focus on a mission that enables training to provide maximum business value.

➤ Command the data you need to make hard choices.

➤ Use business models to shape your new organization.

➤ Structure the new organization around interaction and relationships.

➤ Use business forecasts to scope a new set of offerings.

➤ Integrate, sequence, and orchestrate the transition team's work.

➤ Set and stick to a budget.

➤ Plan for all affected employees to win.

➤ Communicate to meet diverse information needs.

8

Installing: Launch the Training Enterprise

◆◆

Installing is the phase in which you actually create the new training organization and launch its operations. Your transition team will define and develop your initial product offerings; establish effective and efficient processes for relationship management, consulting, publishing, delivery management, and value measurement; create systems for learning technology, knowledge management, and resource management; build your information systems and office infrastructure; select, hire, and train the staff; and initiate your ongoing stakeholder communications. Figure 8-1 illustrates the Installing steps and their position in the broader framework of the transformation to Running Training Like a Business.

Figure 8-1: Key Steps for Installing

PHASES

	ASSESSING	PLANNING	INSTALLING	RUNNING
KEY STEPS	Understand Business Issues, Strategies, and Organization	Scope Full-Scale Operations	Develop and Document Product Offerings, Policies, and Procedures	
	Assess Training Offerings, Processes, People Vs. Best Practices	Map and Structure Future Organization and Relationship	Establish Processes and the Infrastructure	
	Identify Customer Expectations and Level of Satisfaction	Spec the Installation	Select, Align, and Train Staff	
	Conduct Financial/ Vendor Analysis and Technology Assessment	Develop Employee Transition Plan	Implement Employee Transition Process	
	Develop Recommendations, Vision, and CSFs	Develop Organizational Communication Plan	Implement Organizational Communications Process	

131

If it seems to you that Installing is a lot of work, you're right. It's akin to launching a full-blown business. The mental, emotional, and even physical demands may wear on you as the weeks roll on. It's not the kind of challenge you tackle for a mere paycheck: You do it to fulfill a vision.

"It takes high levels of enthusiasm and energy," says Ian Tomlinson-Roe, an HR professional and retail banking area line manager who is co-leading (with Forum's Ellen Foley) the Installing project at NatWest UK. "I have a passion about the management of people. I see this as a rare kind of opportunity to significantly improve a broad range of our people management practices, enhance the capabilities of our employees, and impact bottom-line performance."

Of course, you'll need more than passion for the work to succeed in this phase. Installing is a complex business project in its own right, demanding solid project management skills.

"Our first job as Program Managers is ensuring that the effort is properly structured," Tomlinson-Roe comments. "Ellen and I identify the activity required for a successful installation, arrange resourcing and benefits allocation, track progress against plan, and work with team members to overcome obstacles. We often need to evaluate options and make decisions very quickly. There's not a lot of time to ponder things."

In this chapter, we'll explain how we customarily organize the work required during Installing, offer some thoughts about how best to staff your Installing project, and stress the importance of coordinating the work as it unfolds. Then we'll walk through each of the five main streams of Installing activity:

- Develop and document product offerings, policies, and procedures.

- Establish processes and the infrastructure.

- Align and train staff members.

- Implement an employee transition process.

- Implement an organizational communications process.

Figure 8-2: The Means of Running Training Like a Business

Installing is when you assemble all the means of Running Training Like a Business.

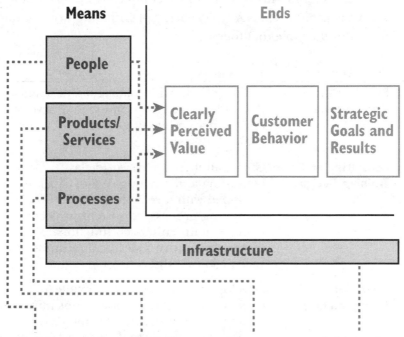

People	Products/Services	Processes	Infrastructure
New staff selected, trained, and aligned with the organization's mission	An initial set of training offerings with participant materials, instructor notes, support materials, course codes, descriptions, and objectives	All key work processes defined and documented	Computers and office equipment, office supplies, and furniture in place
External training resources identified and oriented to the mission of the new training organization	A catalog, calendar, or other literature to describe your offerings, ready for distribution	Operating procedures manuals written, validated, and in use	Telecommunications systems, network connections, modems, etc., installed and operational
Formal management and advisory posts defined and filled		Support services established, including vendor relationships for printing, equipment rentals, hotels, and so on	Information systems and software configured, tested, and fully operational
		Value measurement and reporting systems designed, tested, and deployed	Relevant course, instructor, vendor, participant, HR, and company information loaded into information systems
		Communications vehicles developed and in circulation	

Organizing the Work

Installing will seem far less daunting if you organize the project into distinct *work streams*—major tasks to be completed by certain members of your project team. A typical array of Installing work streams is laid out in the table that follows.

Work Stream	Task Summary
Relationship Management	Build a relationship management team that will ensure that training and development is driven by our customers' business goals.
Consulting and Training Design	Create an integrated, world-class consulting and training design capability, equipped with a reliable and improved consulting process, consistent project management, enhanced functional skills, measurement processes, and business-specific knowledge.
Operations Management	Develop and implement a flexible, effective, and efficient operations infrastructure within the new training organization, using tools such as process maps, flow charts, and functional hand books to ensure that a common language and approach is utilized.
Training Delivery	Establish roles, accountabilities and standards for training delivery. Align and prepare the training team to deliver consistently high-quality training.
Measurement System	Install a robust value measurement system to measure two key aspects of customer satisfaction—process and results—and install a system to measure the total impact of the new training organization based on the Dynamic Business Scorecard.

Production Processes	Create and implement a set of processes and systems that results in direct access to course materials via a centralized repository; best use of staff time, focusing staff on their respective areas of expertise; reducing production time by using pre-qualified, knowledgeable vendors; and materials consistent with the new branding strategy.
Partner Management	Provide a one-stop shop approach to the management of external training suppliers, rationalize the external supplier database, and leverage buying power to obtain the most favorable contract terms for external training solutions.
Knowledge Management	Enable the new training organization to accelerate learning and leverage its collective knowledge through the systematic capture and access of its work, ideas, and expertise.
Technology	Design and implement a strategic IT platform that improves operational efficiency and cost effectiveness, reliability and consistency of data, flexibility in tracking learning activities of all types, production of timely and reliable management information, coordination of work across T&D, and the capability to deliver online learning.
Curriculum	Inventory and assess the current corporate curriculum. Outline the recommended curriculum, eliminate duplication and ineffective proposals, reduce costs, and ensure consistent measurement process and increased confidence in the value of offerings.
Finance	Provide integrated financial systems in support of understanding, monitoring and running the new training organization.

Work Stream	Task Summary
Marketing and Communications	Integrate communication activities within the project team, with the learning and development community, and with the key stakeholders for the new training organization. Develop the value proposition, brand, and branded customer experience for the new training organization, in conjunction with all the key stakeholders.
Resourcing	Create a cost-effective, strategic staff assignment function that will give an organizationwide view of assignments, support customer-applied time targets, create development opportunities, and align with the project delivery process.
Delivery Operations	Develop and install delivery management processes for the new training organization, including systems for registration, class management, participant communications, facilities scheduling, trainer and central supplier communication, materials ordering, and measurement operations.

The work streams cited in the table above will be included in most installations, as they address gaps that typically must be closed to run training like a business. At the same time, most installations will include a few situation-specific streams. NatWest, for example, has a stream called Centres of Excellence, which it has envisioned as "a research and development capability that will establish learning content and processes addressing areas of strategic importance to NatWest across all businesses; creating content which reflects current leading-edge thinking; and focusing on design and development of large-scale initiatives."

During the course of your installation, you may also find yourself adding more work streams, splitting some work streams up into subtasks, or even merging certain streams together to increase efficiency. That's fine. After all, you can't anticipate everything, so stay flexible. Feel free to modify your organization of the work as needed to get it done rapidly and right.

Staffing the Project

Once you've divided the Installing project into distinct streams of activity, you can decide how many people you'll need (and with what mix of abilities) to address each of these vital tasks.

The large-scale Installing projects in which we're typically involved are carried out by a full-time dedicated staff, supported by part-time resources. We prefer to openly recruit for project staff rather than asking management to nominate project team members from within its ranks. Advertising project team openings and interviewing people for all the project positions *seems* time-consuming, but it often saves time over the course of an installation. First, it gives people who are genuinely interested in the work an opportunity to step forward. Motivated people generally work faster than those who would rather be doing something else. Second, recruiting and interviewing candidates for project positions reinforces that these are real jobs. This is an important and thoroughly valid impression to convey. Installing is not committee work to be completed as time permits. Members of your project team should bring to their work all the focus and sense of urgency expected of those in permanent positions. Third, the recruiting process often turns up individuals with unique skills and abilities you'd otherwise overlook. A person with especially strong skills in computers, work process documentation, external resourcing, or telecommunications can save you weeks or even months of effort over the course of an installation.

Recruiting a project team takes diplomacy. True, you've already forecast and justified (in your business case) the cost of the people you need for Installing, and you've won budget approval for those costs (in the Planning phase). Still, some managers are understandably reluctant to let talented employees dedicate half or all of their time to your project. Your recruiting experience will reflect how strong a case you've made for Running Training Like a Business. If you settled for winning "permission" to pursue this sort of change, you'll probably encounter some obstacles. If, on the other hand, you've convinced management that your project will tangibly benefit them and the business, they will be ready to invest in making it happen. That is why you put in all that hard work conducting the assessment and making the business case.

Figure 8-3: Sample Measurement Work Stream Summary

Expected Results	Roles	Solution

• Provide consistent high-quality training across the corporation (measurement instrument: Customer Satisfaction Survey)
• Link training to business strategies (measurement instrument: Customer Satisfaction Survey)
• Measure results of training (measurement instruments: Levels 1-4 measurement tool; ROI stories)
• New training organization report will include:
  • Instructor ratings
  • Course ratings
  • Participant learning
  • Application of learning
  • Impact on business results
• Develop Dynamic Business Scorecard and provide monthly, quarterly, and annual scorecard reports
	• Consulting stream is accountable for training the Consultants on measurement
	• Curriculum stream is accountable for ensuring Level 1 measurement instrument(s) are incorporated into each of the learning offerings, and Levels 2-4 measurement instruments are incorporated where possible (this includes alternative learning deliveries).
	• Delivery Operations stream is accountable for developing a nd installing processes to faciliate the collection and analysis of measurement data.
	• Material Production and Requisition stream is accountable for installing processes to publish and distribute standard measurement tools for each program.
	• Financial stream is accountable for developing and installing the complete financial and accounting systems required to run training like a business.
	• Measurement stream is to ensure integration and consistency of the measurement strategy for transformation program and learning organization, including the development of the Dynamic Business Scorecard.
		• Install a system that measures the two key aspects of customer satisfaction: process and results.
		• **Process**
		  • How well did we function as a team?
		  • Client view of what it was like to work with us
		• **Results**
		  • Satisfaction: Did learners appreciate the experience?
		  • Learning: Has level of knowledge increased?
		  • Behaviors: Are people performing differently?
		  • Results: Have we improved business results?
		• Ensure measurement is baked in to the design process, not bolted on at the end.
		• Create Dynamic Business Scorecard to balance bottom-line measures of the new training organization with customer outcomes and behaviors, internal processes, product and service offerings, and employees.

Specific Deliveries	Measurable Outputs	Date
Defined Dynamic Business Scorecard	• Business Scorecard Report. Distributed monthly, quarterly, and annually to report the results of the new training organization	4/12/99

Defined Measurement Strategy	• Results Chapter in Operations Manual. This chapter will outline the new training organization's measurement strategy and will include documentation of the following:
	  • measurement strategy
	  • standard measurement instruments and reports
	  • measurement processes
		6/12/99

We usually assign one or sometimes two project staff members to lead each work stream. These stream leaders work with the Transition Project Manager to flesh out and clarify the specific tasks and accountabilities for their work stream, to recruit more team members, as needed, and to coordinate the work of their own streams with the work of all the rest.

Figure 8-3 illustrates a Measurement work stream summary, once it has been fleshed out by the stream leader, followed by specific deliverables and due dates for the same work Measurement work stream.

Coordinating the Work

Coordinating the various streams of work may be the most difficult challenge one faces in managing an Installing project, but it is well worth the effort. In fact, it is indispensable. Your streams of work must be integrated.

Delivery Operations, for example, is the work stream through which you create new processes for registration, confirmation, scheduling courses, assigning instructors, and so forth. You might assume that setting up your Delivery Operations would be a relatively simple exercise. But wait—will your Delivery Operations be centralized or de-centralized? What kind of technology could and should you use? How many different kinds of courses should the system be designed to administer? How many different trainers will you need to schedule? Will there be uniform demand for these systems, or steep peaks and valleys at various times of year?

To complicate things further, the answers to most of these questions are still being shaped through the concurrent work of the Technology, Curriculum, and Resourcing streams, among others. In fact, most decisions made in any one stream can have significant consequences for some or all of the rest. Our friends at NatWest call this "the knock-on effect."

As a practical matter, you have to divide Installing into distinct streams of activity. But once you slice up the work, you can't forget that, in practice, the streams aren't truly separate. They overlap everywhere you look. Managing that overlap requires frequent coordination between streams.

"We schedule meetings for people in the various streams to talk to each other at least weekly," reports Ellen Foley. "These aren't just 'come give us an update' meetings, either. There's a lot of cross-stream negotiation. Everyone is adjusting to what everyone else is saying. We structure integration discussions into the project, and then we ask everybody involved to really work at them. You need a lot of give-and-take to make all the pieces of your installation come together."

Such exchanges can be consistently productive, as long as each work stream maintains its focus on the higher goal: bringing the

Figure 8-4: Work Stream "Dashboards"

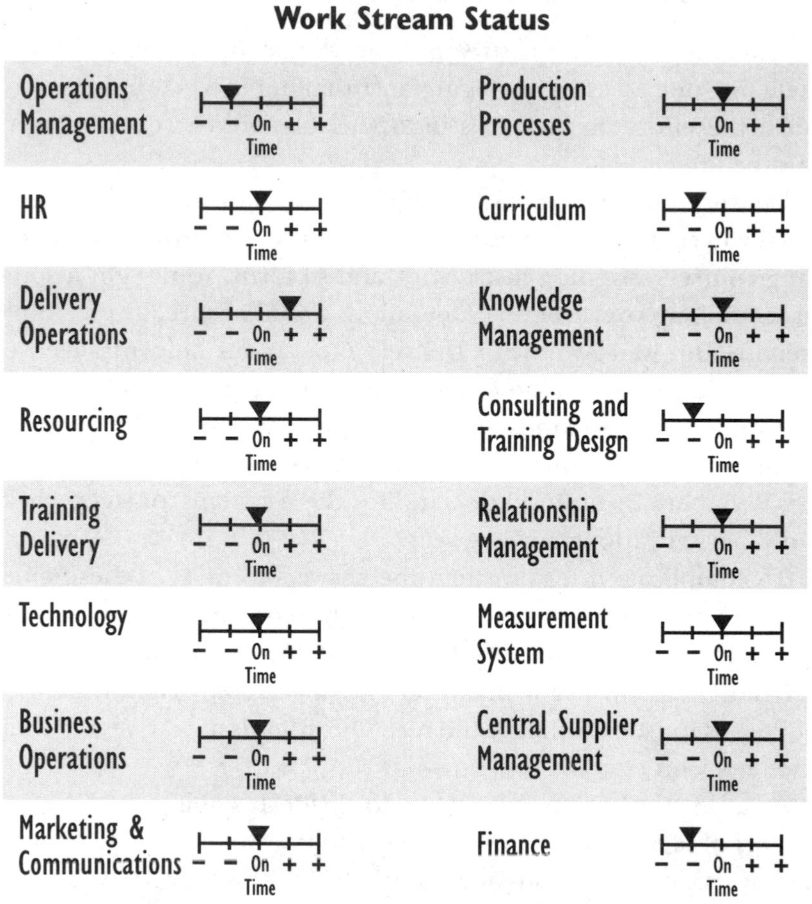

Work Stream Status

Project managers and stream leaders can develop "dashboards" to keep all project team members informed about their progress.

entire Installing project to a successful, synchronized conclusion. If a few work streams falter while the rest forge ahead, the project as a whole may fail. The project team must therefore function *as* a team, even after it splits into distinct streams of work.

Now that you've organized your Installing project into manageable streams of work, staffed the project, and gained everyone's commitment to coordinated effort through teamwork, your team is ready to take the five main actions that will actually create your training enterprise, outlined earlier in the chapter and described in detail in the following sections.

Develop and Document Product Offerings, Policies, and Procedures

Here, briefly summarized, is how we typically go about establishing the new curriculum and initial set of offerings:

1. *Assess Current Offerings*—Essentially, we compile a list of prior and current training services offered. We also identify all courses currently proposed or in development. The thinking here is that we don't want to waste anything that may prove of value to the new training organization.

2. *Recommend New Offerings*—Next, we articulate some criteria consistent with the scope of the new training organization (as defined in the Planning phase) and apply those criteria to shape the recommended set of offerings. For each course or type of training included in the recommended set of offerings, we produce a course profile and course fact sheet—so people will know just what it is we're recommending. As our recommended offerings gain the necessary approvals, we'll start to compile the course profiles into a course catalog.

3. *Run Pilot Sessions*—Just before the official launch date
    for the new training organization, we'll distribute some
    hard copies of the catalog along with an initial sched-
    ule of pilot sessions. We'll put the same information on
    line, and we'll prepare the training materials required
    to run the pilots. At last, the new training organization
    is ready to serve customers! Well, not quite. There are
    still a few other details to address.

Establish Processes and the Infrastructure

Previously, we noted that Processes are a fundamental component of
a complete business organization, as depicted in the Dynamic
Business Scorecard (introduced in Chapter 3.) We've also stated that
a training enterprise requires all the core processes you'd find in a
free-standing enterprise. Figure 8-5 outlines those core processes.

Traditional training functions usually have a defined Delivery
process, of course, but generally lack well-developed versions of the
other core processes required to run training like a business.
Chances are, then, you'll be building most of those processes from
the ground up. At the same time, you'll probably want to overhaul
your Delivery process, to make certain it can satisfy your customers'
heightened expectations. (Hence, streams of work for both Delivery
and Delivery Operations are among our standard components of
Installing.) In sum, the Installing phase is brimming with process
development and process improvement work.

Figure 8-5: Core Processes

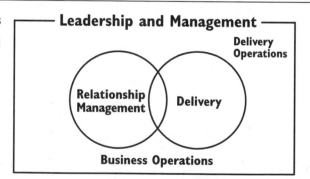

Core Process

- Leadership and
  Management
- Relationship
  Management
- Delivery
- Delivery
  Operations
- Business
  Operations

Let's consider the keys to developing each core process, in turn. Figure 8-6 breaks down the core elements of Leadership and Management.

Figure 8-6: Leadership and Management

Leadership and Management

- Manage training for effectiveness and efficiency
- Establish and manage against business scorecard
- Manage business operations

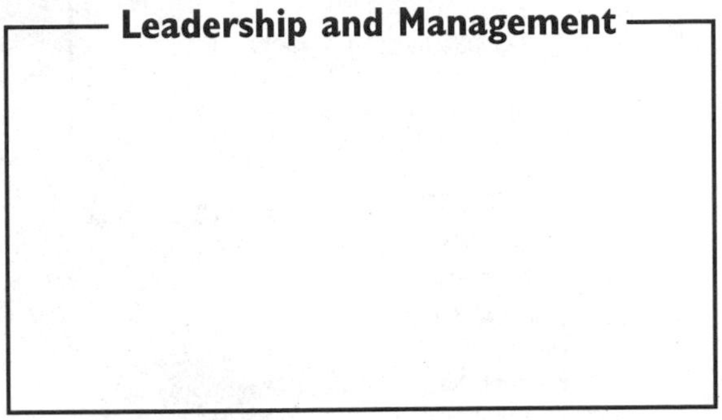

┌─── **Leadership and Management** ───┐
│   │
│   │
│   │
│   │
│   │
│   │
└───────────────────────────────────────┘

In this small space, we can't add much to the body of literature on leadership and management. So we'll simply offer two bywords for determining how to lead and manage your new training organization: *effectiveness* and *efficiency*.

We define *effectiveness* (for our purposes) as "delivering training services that tangibly help businesses to achieve their goals" and *efficiency* as "making your services thoroughly reliable and your true costs clearly evident and highly acceptable to your customers." Effectiveness and efficiency should drive virtually everything one does as a leader or manager of training that runs like a business. We find that consciously managing training against the Dynamic Business Scorecard helps sustain just such a focus.

We also emphasize that the new training organization's managers will have rather substantial operational management responsibilities. It's not enough to be a great trainer or even to lead an organization of great trainers. You also need to ensure that training is a reliable, consistent, and successful business.

Figure 8-7 lists the primary activities within Relationship Management and depicts the core of a relationship management model that has proven effective (as well as highly adaptable) in organizations where training is run like a business.

The Relationship Manager has primary responsibility for identifying opportunities for the training organization to provide value—a

Figure 8-7: Relationship Management

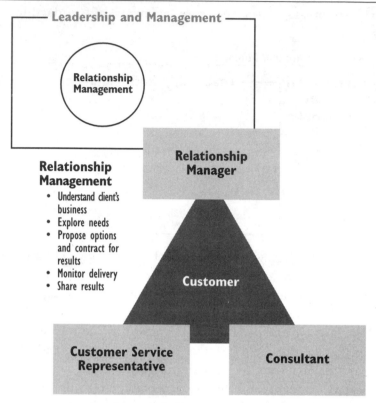

responsibility he or she fulfills more by working with, rather than selling to, the customer.

The Customer Service Representative is often linked to a specific Relationship Manager and assigned to work with the same set of customers to coordinate logistics (facilities scheduling, materials production, instructor communication, billing, and the like) and to generally ensure smooth and efficient fulfillment of all training services.

Consultants, of course, are responsible for the design, development, and (at times) delivery of training solutions, for measuring results, and for capturing key learnings from training experiences. These duties overlap into the Delivery process, which is outlined in Figure 8-8.

Intuitively, you know that linking your Relationship Management process with your Delivery Process is crucial. Otherwise, the training you deliver won't meet the needs identified by your Relationship

Figure 8-8: Delivery

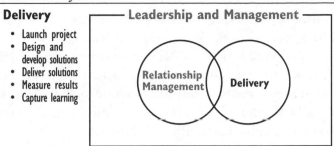

Managers and your customers. But actually bringing these two loops together—especially when the processes are "owned" by corresponding specialists within your training organization—is among the more complex challenges in Running Training Like a Business.

If you chart how it is done by organizations that excel in this regard, a picture of an intricate dance will emerge, one which our colleagues at Forum call the Do-Si-Do. The Do-Si-Do is illustrated in Figure 8-9.

Figure 8-9: Linking Relationship Management and Delivery

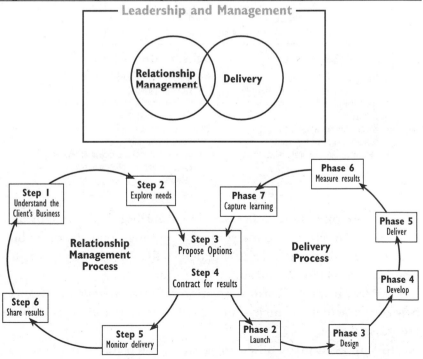

"We purposely shaped our Relationship Management process to get our consultants working directly and substantively with our Relationship Managers and, of course, with the customers themselves," notes Mahbod Seraji of the Moore Learning Alliance. "If I'm a doctor, I don't want to just see lab reports. I want to see the patients, too. It's the same for a consultant whose job is to deliver real business value. They don't want their information to come second-hand. They want to rub elbows with the customer."

Delivery Operations and Business Operations are somewhat less visible but, in the end, no less vital elements of Running Training Like a Business. Figure 8-10 details the main activities for each.

Figure 8-10: Delivery Operations and Business Operations

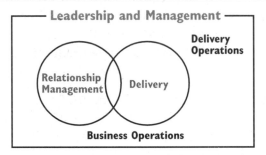

Business Operations

- Manage financial systems
- Analyze and report on business results
- Communicate and market products and services
- Manage Human Resources
- Support information systems
- Administer and coordinate office activity

Delivery Operations

- Register participants
- Schedule facilities
- Communicate with instructors/vendors
- Manage project finances
- Order materials
- Publish materials
- Develop and maintain catalog of offerings
- Establish and maintain a resource network
- Manage participant communications

The core operations processes your transition team designs and installs will largely determine your new training organization's ability to handle the thousand-and-one details that go into being an efficient, as well as effective, training operation.

Granted, it will be hard to envision all those details in advance, before you actually launch your new training operation. But there are ways.

"In this, as in many other areas, we've often found it's better to model your processes on those you find in line businesses, rather than on those you see in traditional training organizations," says Mary Maloney. "You can learn a lot from looking at how a fine hotel, for example, registers and communicates with guests and schedules its facilities. You might benchmark a construction firm's approach to managing project finances, or a weekly magazine for insights on how to publish high-quality printed materials, quickly, under heavy deadline pressure."

Will you be able to launch your new training organization with complete and perfect operations processes? Perhaps not. But that shouldn't stop you from trying. By articulating the core operating processes as thoughtfully and completely as you can—on a micro as well as a macro level—your transition team will provide the new training organization order and substance it may sorely need in the often chaotic days of launching a new training enterprise.

The same is true, perhaps more so, of the office infrastructure. "I don't think a transition team can really claim success," Maloney says, "unless the staff can come in on the first day of operations and find that the phones are actually working, everyone has a suitable place to work, the computers are on the desks, connected and loaded with software and data, the printers, copiers, and fax machines are connected and loaded with paper. . . . Your job is to let them get straight to *work*. You don't want anyone to spend time digging through cartons, looking for a pencil sharpener."

That raises an important lesson we've learned. You need to complete the installation of your new training organization thoroughly before it swings into full-scale operation. And that can be hard, because people may start asking the training enterprise to take on assignments before it is actually open for business. You want to be very clear about what work it can take on, and when.

By the same token, a few early wins can be tremendously beneficial. "In the midst of the Installing phase, you probably won't feel like taking on a training project. It's such a busy time already," says Ellen Foley. "But we've found that, under the right circumstances, it's worth the extra effort.

"A few years ago," she recalls, "we were in the very early stages of an Installing project when we heard from an executive whose division was struggling to break into some new markets. This senior manager believed that his sales force needed some new skills to make the strategy work. Clearly, he couldn't just stand by until we felt all set to serve him.

"So we sent the one experienced Relationship Manager we had on-site in to meet with him. It was a very productive conversation, mainly because they talked about the *business*—what it was trying to accomplish and what it needed to succeed. They combined their perspectives and expertise to define what might be done to quickly raise that sales force's performance. The executive commented, in fact, that it was a different kind of conversation than he was accustomed to having with T&D. He said he wanted us to start work without delay.

"We were able to provide a world-class training response in very short order, tailored to the needs we'd identified with the customer. It was delivered to the entire sales force in that division.

"Several participants commented that it was the best training they had ever received. Many soon reported that the skills they'd learned were helping them to interact with their clients and prospective clients in new, more effective ways. After about three months, the division was beginning to attribute some of its growth in new markets to the new skills being applied by Sales.

"That was certainly the right kind of buzz to have going around the company as we prepared to officially launch our new training organization," Ellen concludes. "Those first few hills seem much easier to climb when you can go at them with some momentum."

In short, we suggest that you quietly look for a few contained opportunities to show customers the possibilities inherent in the larger effort. If you choose those opportunities with care, they can significantly enhance the new training organization's credibility without diluting or delaying your installation.

Select and Prepare the Staff, Implement Employee Transition

If you were to draw your new training organization as the proverbial three-legged stool, the first leg might be your offerings, the second might be your processes, and the third, without a doubt, would be your people. In the Installing phase, your transition team implements its plans for employee transition. This task should be carried out with extraordinary care. After all, you don't want to launch your new training organization with a broken leg.

The most important thing is sticking to the principles that guided your Planning for the staffing and employee transition:

- Select the best-qualified person available for each position.

- Do whatever is necessary to ensure that the transition
  deprives no one of a real chance to go on being successful.

To do both those things well, we've found, you need to articulate and then conscientiously follow an objective process for interviewing and staff selection. Figure 8-11 presents an example of a carefully articulated process checklist.

Everywhere that we've worked through transitions, interviews and selection have been carried out in concert with career planning sessions and, when needed, outplacement services. Our commitment to making every transition a clear win for *every* employee involved, whether they join the new training organization or not, doesn't stem solely from our sense of decency (although we like to think that's part of it). Caring about people and treating them right earns the new training organization some of the goodwill a business must have to succeed.

"I think all of us who were part of the former training function felt we were given a fair shot at being a part of the new training organization, if that's what we wanted," says Gene Cox, who once worked for a major corporation but is now a Forum employee working on an alliance staff. "At the risk of oversimplifying, what the interviewers seemed to be looking for in candidates for the consulting positions were a strong working knowledge of T&D, the usual array of training skills, and intimacy with the businesses. Someone coming in from the outside wasn't likely to have more than two out of three of those qualifications. But, being insiders as well as T&D professionals, we had at least a chance to shine across the board."

Once your staff is selected, your two priorities are to provide whatever training they may need to be effective in their new roles and to

Figure 8-11: Interview and Selection Checklist

Here's an example of a checklist keyed to a carefully articulated process for Interview and Selection.

☐ Select Interview Team	Transition team leader identifies a hiring manager for each open position, and then works with hiring manager to select appropriate interview team (3 to 7 people).
☐ Project Plan	Ensure time has been budgeted for each interviewer in the project plan.
☐ Review and Update Job Description	Transition team leader and hiring manager review job description developed in Planning phase. Update as needed.
☐ Identify Competencies	Transition team leader/hiring manager sends competency list to interviewing team. Each interviewer uses pre-work to pick 3 to 4 job-related competencies under each of the four factors. Transition team leader schedules meeting (either in person or by phone) to facilitate interviewing team in choosing top three competencies for each category. Note: Transition team leader will not move forward with recruiting process until group consensus is gained.
☐ Assign Competency Probes	Use behavioral competencies identified above, and assign probe areas to individual interviewers. Refer to the list of competency probe questions.
☐ Assign Technical Interview	If appropriate, schedule one person on the team to probe technical skills in depth.
☐ Pre-screen Candidates	External candidates: Transition team leader reviews candidates' resumes and performs telephone screens (using behavioral event questioning). Internal candidates will be automatically interviewed face-to-face for open positions. External candidates: Transition team leader/hiring manager screens and selects candidates for interviews.
☐ Conduct Interviews	Transition team leader or employment coordinator will manage all the scheduling of candidates and the interviewing team.
☐ Complete a Balance Sheet	Following every interview, each interviewer completes a balance sheet on the candidate. Completed balance sheets are sent to the employment coordinator for documentation purposes.
☐ Select the Best Candidate	Interviewing team, with the transition team leader, make their decision based on the best fit of each candidate's balance sheet against the Job/Candidate Profile. If two candidates are equal, assign weighted value, then decide who fits best.
☐ Inform All Candidates of Decisions	After a decision is made, the transition team leader will inform all external candidates and thank them for their time. All internal candidates are told of decisions face-to-face either by the hiring manager or transition team leader.

instill a strong sense of team commitment and alignment in your new training organization.

Alignment might be developed through events (for example, off-site team alignment meetings) as well as through ongoing individual and team development plans focused on integrating your new organization, cultivating appropriate organizational norms, and crafting a culture focused on delivering clear value.

Training, of course, must be tailored to the needs of your new staff. If your hiring and selection process went well, most of your staff will already possess the fundamental skills required to perform their duties. Your financial staff will know how to maintain accounts and issue accurate reports. Your Relationship Managers will know how to make contacts and surface customer needs. And your consultants will know how to design, develop, and deliver good training. But all members of your staff will also need to grasp just what is required of them to be successful in your new culture. And for most of them, that culture may be quite different from any they've ever experienced before. They may be new to the world of training, or to the world of business.

"You can't overstate the importance of providing good training, even to people who have a lot of experience in the roles you'll ask them to play," says Cox. "I was an experienced T&D professional, but my job with the newly formed alliance demanded much deeper competencies in sales and customer service. We were and are expected to be an effective part of all aspects of relationship management.

"Today, I'm still delivering training in plant sites across the Southeast," Cox adds, "just as I was in the old days. But back then, my accountabilities were pretty loose—delivering training, facilitating processes, and so on. Now, I'm up against real-world measures—results, costs, revenues. Those numbers get attached to me and my performance. That was an adjustment we all needed some help to make. Fortunately, we got that help, in the form of good training and other kinds of development. The alliance made that investment in all of us, up front, and there's no question it has paid off."

Figure 8-12: A Sample Transition Communication

MOORE FORUM ALLIANCE UPDATE

Volume II • Issue 4   **October 1, 1997**

Alliance Supports New Labels Systems Acquisition
as reported by Dave Allen

A recently completed project for the Labels group and its recent acquisition, Peak Technologies, will enable Peak representatives to enter orders into Moore's manufacturing system. The Alliance account team worked closely with the Labels business unit, Peak management, Moore's National Customer Service Center, and Moore's technology support group to bring this 2-day session to a very successful completion.

Moore Training Providers Move Toward Formal Alliance Relationship
as reported by Cindy Frank and Dave Allen

Activities since our last update regarding contracting with Moore's training providers include:

- a working conference call with Jeff Cowens, President, Seal Group International, leading to a revised final draft being sent for signature
- a working conference call with Larry Rosell, legal, Holden, leading to a revised final draft being sent for signature
- meeting scheduled with Bill Langford and Bob Steed, HRI, to begin contracting process (Tier Two provider)
- discussions with Stevens and Seal Group to develop pricing volume discount for Mike Sinclair's clients in Moore Latin America and Mexico.

On-Line PartNet™ Database Live
as reported by Hugh Howard

Margie White has completed the installation of the PartNet database and the tool is now in place to support the Relationship Managers and Moore clients with requests for solutions to business-related training needs. In addition, the data entry is being used to add new, Moore-specific training providers to the database. The next phase in leveraging this tool will be to develop training around search capabilities for other members of the Alliance.

Implement Organizational Communications Processes

Your communications should convey information that key stakeholders will value while projecting a businesslike identity for the new training enterprise. The newsletter shown in Figure 8-12 (with permission of Moore Corporation) illustrates several qualities worth emulating as you implement your communications strategy. It is homegrown and inexpensive, heavy on news and light on propaganda, brief and to-the-point.

Of course, you'll want to use a variety of media to introduce your new training organization. Keep in mind that using preexisting, familiar business communications channels can reinforce that training is moving more fully into the business mainstream. Above all, try to create opportunities for two-way communications between your staff and key stakeholders.

"We wanted everyone to know everything there was to know about our efforts to improve the efficiency and effectiveness of training," says Paul Earley of Mellon. "We have communicated through Mellon's internal publications, email broadcasts, and flyers to every individual. Every communication reached out, too. We said, 'If you have training needs and want us to try to address them, please let us know.' And I want to tell you, it took some time for people to react. We didn't let up until we started getting calls. We still haven't let up. Our goal is to keep involving the whole organization in shaping our new curriculum."

You'll also want to engage in plenty of face-to-face communication. The leaders of your new training organization need to be highly visible in customer circles, especially at senior levels.

Mahbod Seraji meets monthly with an advisory board composed of the presidents of Moore's business units. "I give them an update on our work, then we talk about what we need to concentrate on," Seraji explains. "The discussion is very informal, very direct, and to-the-point. It's a business meeting, not a dog-and-pony show."

Don't forget to pursue similar kinds of exchanges with stakeholders other than customers. The leaders of training organizations that run like a business all seem to agree: You need strong allies if you

Figure 8-13: New Brand Identity

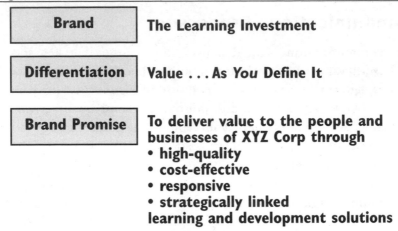

Brand	The Learning Investment
Differentiation	Value . . . As *You* Define It
Brand Promise	To deliver value to the people and businesses of XYZ Corp through • high-quality • cost-effective • responsive • strategically linked learning and development solutions

The Measure of Our Success Is Our Customers' Success

By the time you reach the Installing phase, your communications should include elements rarely seen in those issued by traditional training functions: Brand identity, market differentiation, and a brand promise—as illustrated in this generic example.

hope to make a significant, lasting impact on your customers' business performance.

"We work hard at developing and maintaining our relations with Mellon's HR network, which is highly regarded," says Allen Roberts of Mellon's The Learning Investment. "We want the training we offer to fit hand in glove with HR's strategies. And HR people bring us to the business people out in the divisions. They open doors for us all the time."

Conclusion

By the time you've installed your new training organization, you and your fellow team members will be seasoned entrepreneurs. For the transition you've just completed is, in essence, exactly what one must do to conceive, plan, and then launch any new business.

Traveling this stretch of road takes vision, energy, and perseverance. But it pays you back daily with exhilarating new experiences, countless interim achievements, and an ever-growing certainty that you are making your way to a far better place.

Keys to Successful Installing

➤ Organize the work into manageable, focused work streams.

➤ Consider open posting for project staff positions.

➤ Use diplomacy in recruiting stream team members.

➤ Build in cross-stream integration.

➤ Develop dashboards to track and coordinate progress of work streams.

➤ Get initial set of recommended offerings ready to pilot.

➤ Structure leadership and management to drive effectiveness and efficiency.

➤ Link your Relationship Management and Delivery processes.

➤ Benchmark and model against business (vs. traditional training) operating processes.

➤ Target a few early wins during the Installing phase.

➤ Make the interview and selection process absolutely explicit and highly objective.

➤ Ensure that employee transition is a clear win for everyone involved.

➤ Prepare T&D staff to succeed in a business culture.

➤ Communicate face-to-face and through a variety of media.

PART III

The End
of the Beginning

Now that we've walked through the main phases of the transformation from traditional training organization to Running Training Like a Business, we're ready to look inside the operations of a fully-formed training enterprise.

Chapter 9 highlights what training that runs like a business must do, day after day and year after year, to succeed as a business.

In Chapter 10 a customer shares her perspectives on what it's like to work with a training enterprise.

The Epilogue offers our closing thoughts on Running Training Like a Business and invites others to explore this new frontier.

9
Running: Deliver Unmistakable Value

"This is not the end," Winston Churchill once told his gallant countrymen. "It is not even the beginning of the end. But it is, perhaps, the end of the beginning." That is precisely where this chapter brings us. Through long and diligent effort, your traditional training function has been transformed into a training enterprise. The people, products, processes, and infrastructure required to run training like a business are in place. Any early wins you achieved during the Installing phase have alerted your customers that you are determined to make a difference. It is the end of the beginning. It is time to deliver unmistakable value.

Figure 9-1: Key Steps for Running

	ASSESSING	PLANNING	INSTALLING	RUNNING
KEY STEPS	Understand Business Issues, Strategies, and Organization	Scope Full-Scale Operations	Develop and Document Product Offerings, Policies and Procedures	Lead and Manage the Training Enterprise
	Assess Training Offerings, Processes, People Versus Best Practices	Map and Structure Future Organization and Relationship	Establish Processes and the Infrastructure	Continuously Improve Operations
	Identify Customer Expectations and Level of Satisfaction	Spec the Installation	Select, Align, and Train Staff	Build Customer Relationships
	Conduct Financial/ Vendor Analysis and Technology Assessment	Develop Employee Transition Plan	Implement Employee Transition Process	Design, Develop, and Deliver Training Solutions
	Develop Recommendations, Vision, and CSFs	Develop Organizational Communication Plan	Implement Organizational Communications Process	Measure What Matters

The phases described in preceding chapters were essentially projects, to be completed within a certain number of weeks or months, and all toward completing a transformation of the training function. In contrast, Running constitutes the *ongoing* operation of your training enterprise.

In this chapter, we'll review five main areas—outlined in Figure 9-1—in which a training enterprise must excel, day after day and year after year, to succeed as a business. As we go, we'll tap the experiences of people who are now engaged in Running Training Like a Business, to give you a first-hand feel for the challenges and rewards one might find there.

Lead and Manage the Training Enterprise

Leaders and managers of a training enterprise face a more diverse array of responsibilities than do those who lead and manage traditional training functions.

"You find yourself leading and managing across many different areas and at multiple levels," reports Ed Boswell, General Manager of one of our alliances. "You need all the skills required to run a training staff. But that's just the start. Because you're also managing the multiple functions of a business—Finance, Marketing, Administration. You're negotiating contracts, determining compensation policies, managing quality and cost efficiency . . . And you're doing all those things in between all the time that you spend out and about, being visible, working the organization to find opportunities and to ensure your people get the chance to show what they can do. It's invigorating. And that's a good thing, because there are no slow days in this kind of operation."

"If you want to lead this type of training organization, you'd better know how to fit into a business discussion," says Moore's Denny McGurer. "You want no one to think it's unusual for a training leader to be there in the middle of all the give-and-take. Our goal is for training to demonstrate through its actions that it belongs at the tables where decisions get made. By doing that, we'll earn more credibility for training than any big PR plan ever could."

Money is often at issue. Running Training Like a Business brings all of one's costs out in the open, and training leaders must deal with the resulting sensitivities. For example, some training customers may experience "sticker shock," especially early on. The cost of training is no longer embedded in a corporate budget. Training services that always looked free to line managers are now offered on a pay-for use basis. Lacking experience in such transactions, some customers may be anxious at first about what training costs.

"Pricing projects and setting tuition for the courses we offer is a constant challenge," says Allen Roberts of Mellon's The Learning Investment. "Every time we provide a service, someone has to reach into their pocket and pay us real money. That makes them stop and think. They want to know what they're getting, and they need to feel confident that it's worth paying for."

"Clients may call and ask one of our staff to come out and do some training that individual had been doing for that customer for years," says Boswell. "Only corporate isn't footing the bill any more, so it's my job to say, 'The charge for that service will be $10,000.' That's a tough adjustment on both sides. But listen, these issues are going to arise once you drag your costs out into the light of day. You're going to have to talk with customers about money. We're learning not to be shy about it. Business people can't be."

Sometimes, of course, you're going to be told, "You're not worth $10,000." Leaders of a training enterprise have to help their people get comfortable with having a monetary value assigned to what they can do. In fact, that is just one of many adjustments those who previously worked for traditional training functions must make when moving into a training enterprise. The pressure to perform is palpable. Everyone feels it. It's knowing, "I'm accountable. What I'm expected to do is hard. There's no question, I *could* fail."

"I kid my friends who work in staff positions: 'I don't have a fixed budget. I have to *earn* my living,'" says Mahbod Seraji of the Moore Learning Alliance. "I'm joking, but there's some truth in it. We have to go get our projects. And in carrying them out, we have to use our resources in the best way possible, because at end of month we need to be a successful business as well as a successful training organization."

Once again, we believe Information Technology offers an instructive precedent. These days, IT people don't just talk about bits and bytes. They also talk about profits. They've grown accustomed to being judged on the same terms as any other investment. You can help your people make the same adjustment by managing the training enterprise against a comprehensive business scorecard, such as the Dynamic Business Scorecard we've discussed in previous chapters. You'll then guide your staff toward doing all that's required to deliver unmistakable value to their customers. When you do that, money becomes a much more comfortable topic for all concerned.

The accountability inherent to Running Training Like a Business makes reliable financial management and reporting vital to the training enterprise. You'll need to establish complete and sophisticated financial management and reporting systems such as those listed in Figure 9-2.

Figure 9-2: Financial Management and Reporting

Finance and Accounting Infrastructure

- Expense Reports
- Timesheet
- Profit and Loss Report
- Monthly Closing Work-In-Progress
- Margin Report

Vendor and Client Invoicing

- Vendor Invoice Management Process
- Client Invoice Log
- Contract Log
- Summary Client Invoice

Pipeline Management and Revenue Forecasting

- Pipeline Report Template
- Backlog Report
- Revenue Forecasting Template

Monthly Reporting and Analysis

- Business Scorecard Report
- Monthly Financial Report
- Client Business Unit/Function Coding

Project Financial Management

- Project Costing/Pricing Worksheets
- Pricing Tool Kit Checklist
- Results Contract
- Project Financial Management Forms
- Project Accounting Reports
- Project Financial Management Matrix
- Project Financial Management Process Map

Customers typically require volume data—How much training is going on? How much are we investing?—and of course measurement data—What value are we receiving? Most customers will also look at unit costs. When they perceive that value from training is on the rise and see unit costs for training declining or holding steady, the numbers make them happy.

As you might expect, the managers of the training enterprise covet the same kinds of data—those that document the value training has delivered. For your own purposes, you'll also track revenues, expenses, margins, and other customary measures of business performance. But the data that often prove most valuable are those that help management see ahead. The training enterprise always looks for a glimpse at what's coming. Trends and forecasts help leaders and managers make timely adjustments that optimize your training enterprise's business performance. Figure 9-3 shows two basic examples.

Figure 9-3: Tracking Trends and Forecasts

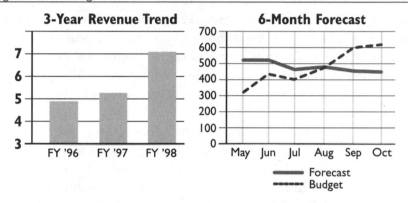

"That's one of the things I like most about managing finances here," notes Chris Allen, Manager of Delivery and Operations for the alliance headed by Ed Boswell. "We don't just crank out numbers. We do a lot of trend analysis. We track 'pipeline' data—the prospects for sales revenue reported by our Relationship Managers—to anticipate what volumes of work the alliance will be handling. And we're always looking at orders, backlog, and the like. The fun part is to put all that data in context—to consider their implications for where our best growth opportunities are, or what resources we might need six months down the road. Sometimes you can look into those numbers and see the future."

Continuously Improve Operations

When a training function is transformed into a training enterprise, big improvements in operational efficiency are almost immediately evident. At Moore, for example, improved resource utilization, more efficient and reliable processes, and aggregated buying contributed to a 35 percent reduction in unit costs for training during the alliance's first year.

"We put a stake in the ground—all vendors that do the work covered under the alliance's charter should work through the alliance, not directly with the businesses," says McGurer. "We said that because it brings a discipline to the process. The alliance offers a results contract and a service guarantee. We feel that's very professional and very legitimate, and there's no reason not to do it. But some providers have balked. We're finding out who wants to play in this league, where you're truly accountable. It's been a real eye-opener."

Mellon instituted a similar policy, asking external suppliers of core- curriculum kinds of training to contract through The Learning Investment.

"It was an obvious and crucial step in our strategy for delivering more consistent messages, through training, across all of Mellon," explains Beth Knobloch, a Mellon vice president. "Still, more than a few vendors fought it. They kept right on going directly to managers out in the divisions. Lately, though, we see external providers realizing that working with The Learning Investment is more an opportunity than an obstacle. After all, we rely on external providers to deliver nearly all of what the alliance offers. Allen Roberts spends nearly all his time working to lead them straight to opportunities in which there's a strongly felt business need, and for which they're well-matched as a training resource. Why fight that?"

The immediate efficiencies gained from Running Training Like a Business certainly do not give the training enterprise the luxury of standing pat. "You launch the new organization with reliable processes for scheduling, registration, resourcing, and the rest already in place, because a business can't afford to run sloppy processes," says Allen Roberts. "But as soon as you've demonstrated an ability to make training work better, faster, and cheaper than it used to, you've raised your customers' expectations. They don't fixate on how swell things *are*. They think about the *possibilities*. That's the nature of customers. They're always looking for you to get better. If you don't, their delight turns into disappointment."

"We see it is as a process of constant adaptation," says Madeline Fassler, Director of Learning for Kaiser Permanente Medical Care Program in California. "I don't think we're ever going to have a model that we'll point to and say, 'That's it! We've found *the* way to do it forever.' Right now we're pushing to leverage our internal expertise while partnering with external experts. That's just today's objective. Things are changing so fast for us, we have to assume that there will always be powerful motivations to adapt and improve our training operations."

"Our basic principles will stay the same, but many of our tactics will change," comments Seraji. "I watch NBA basketball on television. The NBA champion team is the best in the world, but even they modify their game plan throughout each game. They'll stick to certain principles—a fundamental approach they believe in—but their tactical adjustments are constant. We try to make our alliance very consistent yet very flexible, in much the same way."

Where should you focus your continuous improvement efforts? Obviously, the answer is situational. You need to map out your various operating processes, closely monitor their real contributions to delivering unmistakable value to customers, and set your improvement priorities accordingly. Figure 9-4 shows an example of mapping all the way through a macro, value-generating process.

Determining why a project did not meet expectations—yours or your customers'—is usually a matter of finding out which required actions were skipped or poorly executed, case by case. We will, however, venture this one generalization: In our experience, roughly 80 percent of a project's success seems to be determined during the first 20 percent of project work. There's great opportunity in that pattern. By focusing on improving the early elements of each project's life cycle, you'll impose a healthy business discipline on all the work that follows, helping you to realize inordinate benefits in terms of improving your overall operations. These are three early elements on which we focus:

Figure 9-4: Sample Process Map

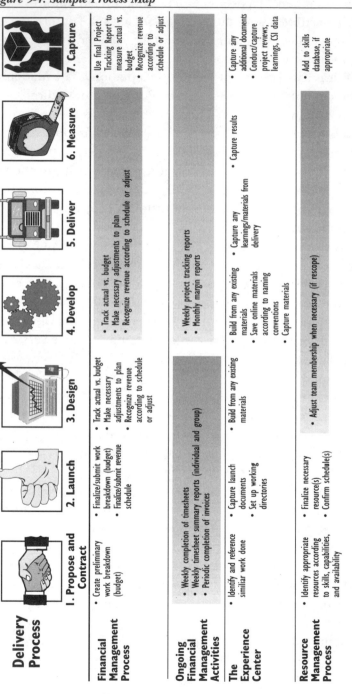

Delivery Process	1. Propose and Contract	2. Launch	3. Design	4. Develop	5. Deliver	6. Measure	7. Capture
Financial Management Process	• Create preliminary work breakdown (budget)	• Finalize/submit work breakdown (budget) • Finalize/submit revenue schedule	• Track actual vs. budget • Make necessary adjustments to plan • Recognize revenue according to schedule or adjust	• Track actual vs. budget • Make necessary adjustments to plan • Recognize revenue according to schedule or adjust			• Use final Project Tracking Report to measure actual vs. budget • Recognize revenue according to schedule or adjust
Ongoing Financial Management Activities	• Weekly completion of timesheets • Weekly timesheet summary reports (individual and group) • Periodic completion of invoices			• Weekly project tracking reports • Monthly margin reports			
The Experience Center	• Identify and reference similar work done	• Capture launch documents • Set up working directories	• Build from any existing materials	• Build from any existing materials • Save online materials according to naming conventions • Capture materials	• Capture any learnings/materials from delivery	• Capture results	• Capture any additional documents • Conduct/capture project reviews, learnings, CSI data
Resource Management Process	• Identify appropriate resources according to skills, capabilities, and availability	• Finalize necessary resource(s) • Confirm schedule(s)	• Adjust team membership when necessary (if rescope)				• Add to skills database, if appropriate

This is an example of mapping all the way through a macro, value-generating process. Remembering why a project did not meet expectations (yours/your customer's) is often a matter of finding out if some required actions were skipped or poorly executed.

- *Defining Deliverables*—When you transform training from a fixed cost to a variable one, you must put a fence around each project. Citing a price for a service without delineating what that service entails (or does not) is like writing the customer a blank check for your resources.

- *Budgeting*—What could be more agonizing than developing detailed budgets for each and every project? Running over budget, repeatedly losing money, or being a great training organization that nevertheless disappoints customers all are considerably worse, in our view. So we develop the budgets.

- *Work Planning*—Do you find yourself saying, "Let's get started. We'll figure out how to staff it later"? We used to say that. (We have the scars to prove it.) Now we stop and figure out who is going to do what, when, and how long it should take. (For an illustration, see the figure titled "Alliance Delivery Macro Process Map" in the Appendix.)

The key to *sustaining* operational improvement across the training enterprise is teamwork, because your performance depends on various specialists successfully blending their efforts over the course of a fairly elongated operating process.

"Once we receive an order, a lot of different tasks have to tie together," says Chris Allen. Chris's group includes a Financial Coordinator as well as Customer Service Representatives (CSRs), who are teamed with the alliance's Relationship Managers.

"The CSRs play a major role in ensuring flawless delivery," he says. "They have lots of direct interaction with customers, answering questions and solving problems. They also work with training participants. CSRs arrange scheduling, registration, materials, and facilities. They're responsible for capturing revenue and for ensuring that customer invoices are accurate, too. You need a broad base of competencies to be a good CSR here.

"When we can work together smoothly, it's good for us, of course, but it's also good for our customers. We try to make every transaction as simple as it can be for them," Chris explains. "For example, the alliance brings in a lot of third-party training providers. We handle all the vendor screening, contracting, and scheduling. We also process the invoices. Our customers get the advantage of being able to bring in multiple providers without taking on any added logistics."

Build Customer Relationships

Ask Mahbod Seraji how to build deep and lasting customer relationships, and he answers without hesitation, "It starts with the Relationship Managers. We have four full-time Relationship Managers on our staff. Their job is to be out there, moving through the customer organizations, so we know just what our customers are after. Understanding their business issues and knowing what they hope to accomplish is step one in creating training solutions that they'll value, which is the only sure way to build the kinds of relationships we're after."

"It's critical that your Relationship Managers not think or act like 'sales reps,'" says Denny McGurer. "They should be out there to listen, first and foremost. The best of them are great listeners who have done their homework. I remember one guy who called on me back when I was still with Kodak. Before he even approached me about sales training, he talked to a Kodak salesperson in Boston and another in Chicago and another in the Southeast. He already knew a lot about my business. He knew what was working well for us, what were our main problems, how fast we were growing, and he had some well-formed ideas about what would influence our success. Other sales people would come in saying, 'I want to be your partner.' But this one already *was* my partner. He'd demonstrated some passion for our business. And he was prepared to offer input of real business value the first time we spoke. Bottom line: He didn't ask for my confidence; he earned it."

Good training and practical tools can greatly increase even the most talented Relationship Manager's chances of building strong customer relationships. We typically equip Relationship Managers with proven but flexible protocols for determining what customers will value, identifying expectations, developing proposals that truly speak to each customer's business issues, and so forth, all the way through contracting procedures, assuring customer satisfaction, and documenting training's business value. Over time, your Relationship Managers should take direct responsibility for modifying and updating those protocols, in light of what they encounter and learn in the marketplace.

"We've learned that you can't treat a customer company as a monolith," reports Ed Boswell. "Our customers are the different business units and the various functions. Some of them want our group to be in constant contact, to wade waist-deep into helping them understand what they need. Others say, 'We just need to hear from you twice a year.' And we have to respect that. There are variations across the board in how customers prefer us to interact with them, so we've had to create a very adaptable organization."

Design, Develop, and Deliver Training Solutions

There *is* an ideal mix of training services. It is defined by your customers. And it changes as regularly as the business environments in which your customers compete. So, in essence, you launch your operations offering the mix that seems best matched to your customers' issues and strategies at that moment in time. Then you never stop adjusting.

The effective shelf life of training materials used to be measured in years, but now they must change much more frequently. You don't have to look far to figure out why. It used to be that corporate structures and strategies were relatively stable, too, whereas today they always seem to be in flux. We don't imagine the business world will go back to its old stable ways soon, if ever. Training that runs like a business not only accepts that reality, it embraces it.

"Our product mix is always changing," Boswell reports. "Right out of the gate, our mix switched from virtually 100 percent open-enrollment courses that you'd choose out of a catalog to just 30 percent open-enrollment courses. The rest was training projects, specific to businesses or functions. Today less than 20 percent of our mix is open enrollment."

Boswell fully expects, however, that his alliance's offerings will always include some open-enrollment courses. "There are plenty of needs out in the businesses that are not attached to specific business issues," he notes. "Basic supervisory and management skills training, for example. In growing businesses, those kinds of core capabilities need to be refreshed year after year, and open-enrollment is an efficient, effective way to get that job done. We're committed, though, to keeping even our standard-type courses fresh and up-to-date with the latest adult learning strategies. We want no part of what we offer to get stagnant."

The training enterprise often shifts quickly from content-driven, open-enrollment course offerings to a mix of projects that match training to the specific needs of a business, as illustrated in Figure 9-5.

At Mellon, the evolution of training's offerings is proceeding more gradually. "We took the core of the training that our headquarters HR function had been providing and turned that accountability over to the new training organization, which we call The Learning Investment. Their charter is to provide a high-quality core curriculum of open-enrollment workshops that cut across all our divisions," explains Beth Knobloch of Mellon. The core curriculum at Mellon includes some PC training and a host of non-technical training offerings in sales, general management, project management, time management, and supervisory skills.

"Our strategy has been to let The Learning Investment sell itself to get into the business lines," Knobloch adds. "We don't push the curriculum on anyone. But we did pilot every single course in the curriculum, and we invited executives to take part in pilot sessions for training that we anticipated would appeal to them, and most of the time, that's what happened.

"In our first year, we had 17 projects that were not expected, where we had senior people decide that they wanted their direct reports to go through the training we'd piloted, with the idea that we'd then work even further down through their line, so they could do some measurement and see where the ROI was coming through. This was a stage we really didn't expect to get to in the first year, but we did. It's something we're really proud of."

"In addition to upgrading and administering the core curriculum," reports The Learning Investment's Allen Roberts, "we've been

Figure 9-5: Sample Activity Report—New Project Activity

Customer SBU/Function	Business Need/ Development Need	Solution (Audience & Activity Level)	% Customized
A/Sales	Develop team-building skills as a result of reorganization in sales group to more effectively meet customer needs and increase sales.	Sales Team leaders from Manager to Regional Directors	10%
B/Technology	Increase interaction, cooperation. Work together more effectively and efficiently to improve product/ development and approval lead time.	Presented five modules of True Teams to 14 participants	10%
C/Sales & Marketing	Improve the skill level of the Sales/Marketing force in a way that will increase both revenue and profitability.	Developed sales and marketing curriculum for 85–90 members of the Sales and Marketing team.	50%
D/Leadership Team	Increase productivity and meet business objectives through better team skills, e.g. reducing the amount of time spent resolving conflicts and communication issues.	Presented selected True Teams modules to VPs and Business Managers.	60%
E/Sourcing	Sourcing upgraded their desktop equipment to the Windows 98 format. The business need was to train the sourcing people on the Windows 98 and Word, Excel, and PowerPoint software.	500 participants in a customized Windows 98 course to meet their specific needs.	100%
Corporate/Legal	Increase reading comprehension to process backlog of records management.	Presented reading comprehension training to 17 Records Analysts and Supervisors.	50%
F/Retail Sales	Division F acquired several retail businesses in 1997. The salespeople in these businesses needed to improve their sales skills.	Presented face-to-face selling skills programs with custom role plays for 150 employees.	20%
G/Distributor Relations Group	Improve business acumen of distributors on financial aspects of their businesses.	Presented financial programs for 20 Division G distributors	30%
H/Administration	Division G upgraded their desktop to the Windows 98 format. The business need was to train all the Administration people on Windows 98 and Word, Excel, and PowerPoint software.	Windows 98 Getting Started presented to 200 participants.	100%

asked to 'continuously assess training needs,' which often boils down to searching for ways to make training more strategic. Maybe a fourth of what we did last year was explicitly linked to some part of the bank's strategic agenda. Eventually, we may see that ratio reversed, with only 25 percent of our offerings being plain vanilla and 75 percent serving some business-specific need. Our opportunities to make training more strategic will increase as we prove ourselves by demonstrating to the bank's divisions that we can help them get results."

Sometimes, the line to results is very direct: The training enterprise perceives a skills gap and moves to fill it. The Learning Investment at Mellon, for example, found a strongly felt need for enhanced presentation skills and responded with a tailored Presentation Skills Workshop.

"The participants said 'Wow! This is great!' because the workshop was structured around the presentations they actually give, day in and day out," recalls Roberts. "They were excited because they knew this would make them more effective with their customers. Some participants then asked us to help them improve their presentation materials as well as their skills. So we hooked them up with one of our best vendors, and we aligned their materials with the new approaches they'd learned in the workshop. One training experience can definitely change things for people in a business."

The business impact of training doesn't have to be immediately evident, however, to be unmistakably valuable. "Mellon's Retail Financial Services business has set out to be the premier retailer in that very competitive arena of the banking business," Roberts says. "They've invested heavily in technology. Now they want to focus on building a culture that's more consistent with their strategic objectives.

"We're working on a process with Retail Financial Services' top 70 executives," he continues. "These are very talented, very successful people who were objective enough to say, 'Most of us got where we are on the strength of our banking skills. We don't know all there is to know about building a world-class retail culture.' We've proposed a series of workshops which will be reinforced by regular monthly meetings. We'll introduce them to a set of directly applicable strategic tools, and we'll conduct some 360-degree feedback to help them track how they're doing.

"This kind of goal—changing a business culture from that of a traditional bank to that of a modern retail venture—is achieved gradually, and we're just playing a part in the very beginning," Roberts notes. "But our customer can see that we're giving them a big start in a direction that they themselves say could lead Mellon to preeminence in retail banking."

At Moore, the new training organization was launched in August 1997 with an unequivocally strategic mandate to "support Moore divisions in the achievement of Direction 2000 goals and business plans."

Mahbod Seraji reports that the Moore Learning Alliance's offerings have been shaped principally by four of Moore's most crucial business imperatives:

- Make the sales force more productive.

- Improve sales management and sales operations.

- Use integrated scorecards, to guide and measure more integrated efforts to increase employee satisfaction, productivity, customer satisfaction, and profits.

- Increase overall effectiveness of first-line management (supervisors).

"How did we decide that our training offerings should address these priorities? We sat in on management meetings, especially those in which the topic was how to achieve Moore's Direction 2000 goals," Seraji explains. "Moore's line managers said these four objectives are among the keys to their business success, so we took them as our marching orders." Halfway through 1998, Moore's new training organization reported that 67 percent of its engagements were targeted to meet a specific corporate goal. Ninety-four percent were targeted to meet a stated business goal.

Training organizations that run like a business also need to stay quite flexible about *where* the training they offer is developed. Most create at least some of their offerings themselves and draw from other training suppliers whenever that proves more practical.

The Moore Learning Alliance, for example, maintains a staff of four talented consultants capable of developing many new training offerings. But rather than building its "Developing High Performers" management training from scratch, the alliance decided to adapt from an existing program that had been created by Moore's old T&D function. The alliance has also turned to external providers to develop order-entry training (via the Internet), as well as to custom-develop training in Moore Value Analysis™ software.

"We don't think it's inherently better for us to make or to buy training for our customers," says Seraji. "It depends entirely on the customer's business needs, on what training is or is not available to address those needs, on the size and makeup of the targeted training population, on the scope of your training mission, and on the economics of the specific situation. These are the factors that you must weigh to decide if one option is truly better than another."

Veterans of Running Training Like a Business readily admit that economics plays a large part in their decisions regarding what training to offer and how to source it.

"Let's say that over 18 months, you've gone out and delivered a specific set of training—an offering that you developed in-house—to a large training population and it has proven very effective," Ed Boswell says. "But shortly after you wrap up that project, your customer hires one new person with the same learning need. Going back out to deliver that training again to a population of one is not cost-effective. In those cases, our customers and we often agree to steer that individual toward an open-enrollment option. It's not ideal, but it makes sense in cost-benefit terms, because that person will get 60 percent, 70 percent, or 80 percent of the learning he needs for perhaps a tenth of the cost. It's a business-like decision."

There are times, though, when economics can be overridden by other considerations. "Part of the lore around here is a story we call 'Fix Fred,' because that was what the manager who phoned us asked us to do," Boswell says. "Fred was struggling with people management. In strictly economic terms, this manager was clearly a candidate for open enrollment, because he was the only one we were being asked to help. But as we looked into Fred's needs, we saw that a standard course might not do the job. So we put together some training that would go straight to his specific opportunities for improvement.

"As it turned out, that approach even worked out in economic terms," Boswell recalls. "A Relationship Manager on our staff made a few calls and found out that Fred's needs weren't so unique, after all—at least, not in certain parts of the corporation. We turned up about 30 other managers who could benefit, then we ran the training. It was cost-effective, Fred got 'fixed' and he didn't feel singled out anymore. It was a happy circumstance where our mandate to be cost-efficient and meet our customers' specific needs all came together."

Ed's story illustrates that, when Running Training Like a Business, one can't equate "efficiency" and "consistency" with rigid adherence to strict policies and procedures. Sure, you need to set and stick to clear methods and standards. But you also have to allow that the most efficient solutions sometimes stem from being extraordinarily flexible and innovative in responding to customers' needs.

In sum, a training enterprise's offerings are not shaped by what its staff happens to be good at, by what courses it happens to already have listed in a catalog, or even by what kinds of training its customers valued in the past. Its offerings are shaped to help customer organizations and their people succeed in business, now and in the future. Every other consideration is secondary.

Measure What Matters

When training runs like a business, measurement isn't a cause. It's a given. Measurement permeates everything. And everyone is involved. But the people in your training enterprise should approach measurement with purpose, not fervor. It is an integral part of their jobs, nothing more and nothing less.

That doesn't mean training that runs like a business is complacent about measurement. Far from it. "You want the training organization to have certain goals and results that it has targeted, and you want its people to go after those targets with ambition, just as people will in any high-performing business," says Richard Harris, a Forum authority on measurement. "Ideally, the people of the training organization will pay attention to and work at measurement because it conveys information that's important to them. Measurement should be an indispensable key to fulfilling their ambitions. It should also show them that they are accomplishing what they set out to accomplish."

We've found that it is almost always a waste of time to push people into a measurement system, especially one you started just because some boss or customer is beating you up on the measurement issue. People simply won't stick with measuring something that isn't important to them.

In training that runs like a business, everyone has significant and specific measurement responsibilities. The following table outlines the measurement responsibilities of various members of the training enterprise.

Role	Responsibility
Relationship Manager	• Identifies client needs and the results expected. • With the client, determines the level of measurement required. • Documents the measurement requirements on the Client Expectations Sheet. • Reviews project evaluation and measurement as documented on the results contract and secures client authorization for the project. • Prepares Project Follow-up Evaluation with client at the conclusion of the project, if a Client Satisfaction Questionnaire was not used on the project. • Reviews results with client at the conclusion of the project.
Project Leader	• Develops the measurement strategy for the project and designs instruments, as needed. • Facilitates a meeting with the client team to develop the Client Satisfaction Questionnaire and forwards the metrics selected to performance measurement database.

- Reviews results with clients throughout the project and takes follow-up action as required.
- Sends summary of measurement report on project to Managing Director, Relationship Managers/Capability Development
- Analyzes measurement data and prepares client report.
- Meets with Relationship Manager and client to review results.
- Reviews data with project team at the capture meeting.

Customer Service Representative (CSR)

- Sends measurement instruments to instructors as part of the instructor briefing package.
- Reviews measurement requirements with instructor.
- Inputs Level 1 participant and instructor evaluation results into training server.

Instructor

- Tees up measurement at the beginning of the training and administers pre- and post-testing, if required.
- Directs participants to complete Participant Satisfaction Questionnaires and sends them to performance measurement database.
- Completes an Instructor Feedback Form and returns it to the CSR.

Administrator

- Assists Financial Coordinator with preparation of monthly Dynamic Business Scorecard.

Managing Director, Relationship Managers

- Prepare monthly summary of Level 2, 3, and 4 data and send to Financial Coordinator.

Financial Coordinator

- Captures data on client satisfaction, budget and timeliness on contract log from Customer Satisfaction Index and Follow-up Project Evaluation.
- Prepares monthly business and financial reports.

In a training enterprise, then, the Running phase is marked by ongoing measurement decision making in which *everyone* takes part. We focus on these three basic elements of measurement decision making:

- Deciding *what* is important enough to measure (that is, What really matters?)

- Deciding *how* to measure those important aspects of your operations (that is, choosing your metrics)

- Deciding *who* will take responsibility for each aspect of measurement

Most training measurement systems should include measures that gauge Kirkpatrick's Levels 1 and 2 of impact. (The Kirkpatrick model was discussed in Chapter 2.) Our general philosophy, though, is that training should push out to measure Levels 3 and 4 whenever possible.

Essentially, we'd urge you to approach each measurement activity with the intent of showing that training "moved the needle" on whatever it is that the customer wanted—increased customer satisfaction, reduced cycle time, cost savings, or increased sales, for example.

It can be done. Here, for example, are some of the measured impacts recently reported by one of the training enterprises with which we've been associated:

- *Increased Revenue*—A $20 million increase in revenue helped, in significant part, by a strategic marketing intervention, in which the SBU invested $375,000

- *Enhanced Operations*—Improved first-pass yield to more than 85 percent, improved uptime by 3 percent, set worldwide production records and slashed customer complaints to 50 percent of monthly target through the implementation of a customer-focused, high-performance work system at this unit's North American plant site

- *Improved Employee Satisfaction*—Achieved 95 percent overall employee satisfaction (up from 80 percent) in a North American business region following intensive senior management development work over an 18-month period

- *Customer Retention*—Supplier of the Year award from GE and recovery of 30 percent of this unit's total revenue, attributed by management, in significant part, to an intervention focused on effective communication and collaborative problem-solving with the customer

- *Asset Productivity*—A 5 percent increase in worldwide production with no new capital investment, due in significant part to changes one unit's leader implemented while participating in a Leadership for Growth program

True, many times you won't be able to document business impact at such levels. That's something all of us in training must accept. What we can't accept is the failure even to try. The cost to the training profession's credibility is simply too high, and the untapped opportunities to convey unmistakable value are too great, for anyone in training to be satisfied with the status quo in training measurement.

Conclusion

We know of just a handful of training organizations that fit our concept of Running Training Like a Business. Yet already a remarkable variety of approaches has emerged within the concept. The missions one training enterprise tackles can be strikingly different from those taken on by the next. Some training enterprises are quite large, as training organizations go, while others maintain but a few full-time staff. The products and services training enterprises offer are as diverse as the customer bases they were conceived to serve.

Still, all training enterprises share at least this one characteristic in common: Each gauges its performance not against some abstract standard, but against the tangible business value it provides to customers. And that, in the end, is what we really mean by Running Training Like a Business.

Keys to Successful Running

➤ Broaden leaders' and staff members' spectrum of
   accountabilities.

➤ Don't fear talking about money.

➤ Stay visible at senior levels of customer organizations.

➤ Fit into business discussions.

➤ Structure and manage the enterprise for operational
   efficiency.

➤ Map and monitor your operating processes' contributions to delivering clearly perceived value.

➤ Maintain consistent principles but make constant
   tactical adjustments.

➤ Focus improvement efforts on the front end of training
   projects.

➤ Tailor relationship management to each customer's
   preferences.

➤ Give Relationship Managers proven but flexible
   protocols to follow.

➤ Never stop adjusting your mix of training offerings.

➤ Structure pilots to showcase your value potential.

➤ Help customers achieve long-term as well as immediately
   achievable objectives.

➤ Apply business rationale to "make vs. buy" decisions.

➤ Make training content genuine and relevant to
   participants.

➤ Make training a two-way street for the customer business and its employees.

➤ Push for measures that document training's business impact.

10
A Customer's Perspective
◇◇

As we were finishing work on this book, we invited a training alliance customer, Susan Christie, Vice President of Sales Operations for Moore North America, to share her perspective on training that runs like a business. Here's what she told us:

> Your book says, "Training should address the customer's issues and strategies at that moment in time." *I* say, "Nothing less will do." Not in our world.
>
> The Sales Operations group, located in Lake Forest, works closely with Moore's North American Sales organization as well as the Moore Learning Alliance. Our job is to make sure the structure, strategy and training all come together to help us optimize the unique strengths that differentiate Moore from the competition. The industry as a whole is experiencing great change, and our customers' expectations are changing as well. Moore is creating a very different organization to meet these challenges, lead the industry, and better serve our current and future customers. I tell you this because it's important to understand: *That's* the environment here. All of us in Sales and Sales Operations are very excited about what we're doing. We must be able to move very quickly and our partners must do the same.
>
> Okay. You have the background. Here's the story I want to tell.
>
> In August 1998, Moore moved to a North American structure, which meant collapsing three areas and eleven divisions into eleven geographic regions covering the U.S. and Canada. John McDonald, VP of Sales for Moore North America, named 11 Vice President/General Sales Managers (VP/GSMs) to run these new regions. Each would have full P&L responsibility.

We'd never done that before. Moore Sales Managers had traditionally been responsible for revenue and gross profit, but never for all the factors that ultimately drive the bottom line. John felt strongly that the management team must have full P&L responsibility to execute the Moore North America strategy and drive the necessary change in the shortest amount of time.

This new Vice President/General Sales Manager position was the kind of responsibility that anybody who's good at Sales Management would want. It's a terrific job and a great challenge. Strong managers often wonder, "How much could I accomplish if I really had the chance?" Well, here was the chance. Our challenge was to provide the right training and tools to support the new responsibilities.

Each VP/GSM had already achieved many career milestones. What most had not done was manage a true profit-and-loss business. They needed a good, practical P&L skill set. That much was clear. They would also be challenged to provide extraordinary leadership to a sales organization that was experiencing tremendous change. Somehow, we had to help the VP/GSMs quickly develop this broad set of crucial skills. Within 30 days, in fact.

We contacted our Relationship Manager from the Moore Learning Alliance. In one two-hour meeting, we outlined the objectives and shared ideas on how to get this job done. John McDonald envisioned an intensive five-day training session. We traded some thoughts on how to focus and structure the training, then asked the alliance to give us a proposal.

A few days later, the alliance came back with a plan for a five-day learning experience, which they called the "Vice President/General Sales Manager Learning Institute." It addressed the full range of P&L and leadership skill sets we required. It did other things, as well. There was a good amount of planning built into the agenda, so the participants would leave the institute not only with skills, but also with a clearer understanding of what they'd be doing in their new roles. The training also focused on open communication and team building. Both those emphases later proved very important and extremely valuable, to the new VP/GSMs and to Moore as a corporation.

We were especially intrigued by the alliance's recommendation that we weave a computer simulation through the five-day course. Our Relationship Manager had spoken some weeks before to a training partner called Strategic Management Group (SMG) that had developed an interactive business simulation. When he heard what we were trying to accomplish, he made the connection and went back to take a closer look at the simulation. It was a good fit. The alliance proposed that teams of three or four VP/GSMs work through the simulation together to manage a fictional manufacturing company in pursuit of profitable, long-term growth.

We made a few adjustments to the plan and we were ready to go. Working very collaboratively with the alliance, we had pulled together what we felt would be a best-in-class training effort in record time.

The training was intense and fast-paced. It immersed us in new perspectives and required us to think and work in new ways. A guest speaker outlined five customer-centered strategies for growing a business. We later assessed our own organizations around the practices associated with those strategies. We learned the fundamentals of managing to a P&L as well as targeted leadership skills, then applied them in the simulations. All through the week, we were building on a base of knowledge.

The simulation confronts you with a rapidly changing company and marketplace. That's just what we face everyday. As you work through it, the simulation presents you with a *lot* of opportunities. The experience of discussing and then making these real-time decisions, while immediately seeing the probable *long*-term impact was a tremendous learning experience. It changed our business decision-making behavior.

I've seen a huge change in how we think. We're asking ourselves, Is this a good business decision longer term? Would I take this at the expense of something else? It's taking into account that every choice is going to cost me an alternative. If I do this, what will it cost us in terms of focus? We've moved to a more balanced decision-making process. We still move fast, but we don't rush. We're much clearer about how our decisions will impact the business.

This training prepared the VP/GSMs for the responsibility of running and growing a profitable business. It rolled all aspects of that responsibility together—doing what's good for the customer, for the company, and the region. The feedback from the VP/GSMs was very positive. Every one rated the experience at 4.5 or higher on a 5-point scale. And these are not people who are easily impressed.

The payback on our investment in the institute is enormous. It comes in the form of sound business decisions, the kind that pay off in profitable growth. The institute also fostered a tremendous sense of teamwork. One of the most significant benefits I saw over the five days was the breaking down of silos and barriers. It built a common understanding that, to be successful, we have to work together. When you pick up the phone and your counterpart says, "Tell me what you need," instead of "That's not my responsibility," there's a huge difference in what you can do.

We're now planning a four-day version of the institute for our entire North American Sales Manager group. This will align the entire management team and create powerful change. From an operating standpoint, we're going from running a relay race, where one person runs at a time and then passes the baton, to something more like a rugby scrum, where we're all running down the field at the same time, throwing the ball back and forth. I heard that metaphor years ago, and it describes the change we're effecting today.

The institute represents the best of what you're talking about in your book. Yes, T&D must address the basics. Every organization, including Moore, must build skill sets, year in and year out. But from my perspective, the real power of the alliance is when we can say, "Our environment is changing quickly and we need to respond immediately with the appropriate skill set development." We have a partner we can collaborate with to create a great solution in record time. This is real value.

Thank you, Susan. Your story illustrates that a training organization *can* possess all the business insight, capabilities, and flexibility needed to deliver value as its business customers define it, however they define it. That's the great payoff from Running Training Like a Business. That's what makes all the hard work that goes into building a training enterprise more than worthwhile.

Epilogue

Back in the Preface, we asked you to consider how satisfied you are with the return on your investments in training (whatever form those investments may take). Since you've read this far, we'll assume that you sensed room for improvement. Now what?

Apply your understanding of Running Training Like a Business to gain a sharper perspective on the T&D organization that serves *your* business. Here's a simple self-assessment tool we've long used to capture such perspectives from members of training organizations, and from executives whose businesses are served by T&D. We suggest you take a few moments to rate your training organization against these criteria. Better yet, invite a few others to do the same, so you can compare your perceptions.

Differentiating Characteristics of a Training Enterprise	Your Perception: Rate the Extent to Which Each Phrase Describes Your T&D Organization	1 = Little/No Extent 4 = To Some Extent 7 = High Extent
Business Linkage	Hardwired to strategy and key business issues	1 2 3 4 5 6 7
Measurable Impact/ROI	Measured by its impact and return on investment	1 2 3 4 5 6 7
Quality	Relevant and of consistently high quality	1 2 3 4 5 6 7
Speed and Responsiveness	Moves as quickly as the business needs it to, responds to specific business needs	1 2 3 4 5 6 7
Cost Effectiveness	Costs are leveraged and commensurate with value derived	1 2 3 4 5 6 7

Differentiating Characteristics of a Training Enterprise	Your Perception: Rate the Extent to Which Each Phrase Describes Your T&D Organization	1 = Little/No Extent 4 = To Some Extent 7 = High Extent
Pay for Use	A variable cost to users . . . they pay only for what they use	1 2 3 4 5 6 7
Leveraging Resources	Accesses and leverages the right resources to meet customer needs	1 2 3 4 5 6 7
Access and Service	Provides a clear point of contact and high level of service for customers	1 2 3 4 5 6 7
Accountability	Provides clear accountability for efficiency and impact of the work	1 2 3 4 5 6 7
Operational Excellence	Utilizes efficient and effective systems and processes	1 2 3 4 5 6 7
Competitive Advantage	Makes tangible and significant contributions to the business's competitive advantage	1 2 3 4 5 6 7

Total of points awarded = _____

What do your ratings mean? Here are some guidelines for interpreting the score you gave to your training organization, based on what we've learned from delving deeper into businesses that began by completing similar self-assessments. Generally speaking, when the total of points awarded T&D in initial self-assessments falls between:

11 and 44 We subsequently find widespread and significant opportunities to increase the value returned on the training investment.

45 and 64 We find that T&D is doing many things right, but that there are still plenty of attractive opportunities to generate more tangible business value from training.

65 and 77 We've rarely encountered an initial assessment score this high. If you awarded your training organization more than 65 total points, please contact us. We want to benchmark you!

Is this self-assessment scientific? Hardly. Illuminating? Almost always. It often provides business and training people alike their very first glimpse of their training organization against the standard of Running Training Like a Business. And that's bound to shed some light.

If the potential for T&D to generate more business value seems significant, you'll want to actively consider your options for pursuing that opportunity. Those options range beyond those we've described in these pages, by the way. The handful of training functions that have pursued Running Training Like a Business thus far have certainly established that something is *there*—something substantial and full of promise. And each time another training organization ventures out in this new direction, we learn more. But it will take many years to fully chart the best routes and identify the full potential of Running Training Like a Business. The process of exploration has just begun.

We're optimistic that it will continue. The motivations to explore this realm are the very same motivations that drive people to explore all the frontiers of business—the motivation to grow, to make a difference, and to be successful.

If such motives drive you, and if you feel that Running Training Like a Business could make T&D a more valued part of your business, don't hesitate. Explore the possibilities! You invest so much in training. You owe it to your business, and to yourself, to ensure that training provides unmistakable value in return.

Appendix

Scoping Questionnaire

The Scoping Questionnaire is used primarily in the Planning phase.

Initially, it is used by the Transition Project Leader to estimate the length of the transition, to define the size and capability requirements for the transition team, and to forecast what other resources may be required to successfully complete the project.

The Scoping Questionnaire is subsequently used by the entire transition project team to develop a clear understanding of the current state of T&D, shape and scope the new training enterprise, and identify specific gaps between current resources and capabilities and those required for the future.

Offering	Current State	Alliance Scope
	1. Check current training organization offerings: ☐ Individual development open enrollment courses ☐ Corporate initiatives ☐ Business-specific projects ☐ Public seminars (one-offs) ☐ Certification ☐ Licensing ☐ Tuition reimbursement ☐ Other:_____	**1. Check proposed alliance offerings:** ☐ Individual development open enrollment courses ☐ Corporate initiatives ☐ Business-specific projects ☐ Public seminars (one-offs) ☐ Certification ☐ Licensing ☐ Tuition reimbursement ☐ Other:_____
	2. Check current categories of training offerings: ☐ Customer Industry Knowledge ☐ End-User Computing ☐ Finance and Accounting ☐ Human Resources and Union Relations ☐ Health, Occupational and Environmental Safety ☐ Information Systems and Technology (Technical) ☐ Licensing and Certification ☐ Management and Leadership Development ☐ Marketing ☐ Products and Services ☐ Procurement ☐ Project Management ☐ Professional Development and Productivity ☐ Quality ☐ Sales ☐ Service Excellence ☐ Technical ☐ Technical Operations	**2. Check proposed categories of alliance training offerings:** ☐ Customer Industry Knowledge ☐ End-User Computing ☐ Finance and Accounting ☐ Human Resources and Union Relations ☐ Health, Occupational and Environmental Safety ☐ Information Systems and Technology (Technical) ☐ Licensing and Certification ☐ Management and Leadership Development ☐ Marketing ☐ Products and Services ☐ Procurement ☐ Project Management ☐ Professional Development and Productivity ☐ Quality ☐ Sales ☐ Service Excellence ☐ Technical ☐ Technical Operations

Offering	Current State	Alliance Scope

	3. Indicate by # and % the current intellectual property mix:
	
	               # %
	
	In-house _____ _____
	
	External _____ _____
	
	Total _____ 100%
		3. Indicate by # and % the planned intellectual property mix:
		
		               # %
		
		In-house _____ _____
		
		Partner(s) _____ _____
		
		3rd parties _____ _____
		
		Total _____ 100%

	4. Indicate the # and % of in-house courses that have:
	
	             # %
	Participant
	materials _____ _____
	
	Instructor
	materials _____ _____
	
	Stuff Lists _____ _____
	
	Collation
	sheets _____ _____
	
	Total _____
		4. Indicate the # and % of alliance courses to have:
		
		             # %
		Participant
		materials _____ _____
		
		Instructor
		materials _____ _____
		
		Stuff Lists _____ _____
		
		Collation
		sheets _____ _____
		
		Total _____

	5. Indicate the # and % of vendor courses that have:
	
	             # %
	Participant
	materials _____ _____
	
	Instructor
	materials _____ _____
	
	Stuff Lists _____ _____
	
	Collation
	sheets _____ _____
	
	Total _____
		5. Indicate the # and % of vendor courses to have:
		
		             # %
		Participant
		materials _____ _____
		
		Instructor
		materials _____ _____
		
		Stuff Lists _____ _____
		
		Collation
		sheets _____ _____
		
		Total _____

Offering	Current State	Alliance Scope
	6. List courses which will need to be delivered/ redesigned immediately (state reason): – – –	**6. Identify which courses will be redesigned as part of the Transition project (T) and those which will be initiated separately as a Fast Start project (F):** – – –
	7. Are there inventories of materials? ☐ Yes ☐ No If yes: Where?_____ _____ _____ How much?_____ _____ _____ Why?_____ _____ _____	**7. Inventories will be:** ☐ Just in time ☐ Maintained until depleted ☐ Other:_____

Offering	Current State	Alliance Scope
	8. Indicate the delivery method by # and % of participant hours: 　　　　　　# 　　% Instructor led ＿＿＿ ＿＿＿ Self-study ＿＿＿ ＿＿＿ Lab/Mini-module ＿＿＿ ＿＿＿ Computer-based ＿＿＿ ＿＿＿ On-the-job training ＿＿＿ ＿＿＿ Other: ＿＿＿ ＿＿＿ Total ＿＿＿ 100%	**8. Indicate the delivery method by # and % of participant hours:** 　　　　　　# 　　% Instructor led ＿＿＿ ＿＿＿ Self-study ＿＿＿ ＿＿＿ Lab/Mini-module ＿＿＿ ＿＿＿ Computer-based ＿＿＿ ＿＿＿ On-the-job training ＿＿＿ ＿＿＿ Other: ＿＿＿ ＿＿＿ Total ＿＿＿ 100%

People	Current State	Alliance Scope
	9. Current T&D staff understanding of the purpose of this project: (Check all that apply)	
	☐ Link training to strategies and key business issues	
	☐ Measure training impact on business and return on investment	
	☐ Reduce the total cost/ investment	
	☐ Reduce the unit cost of training (per person per day)	
	☐ Convert fixed costs to variable (pay for use)	
	☐ Provide clear accountability for operational efficiency and impact of work	
	☐ Increase responsiveness and speed	
	☐ Provide consistent high-quality training across the corporation	
	☐ Implement alternatives to classroom training	
	☐ Increase efficiency and effectiveness of T&D operations	
	☐ Access and leverage right resources for needs	
	☐ Other:_____	
	☐ Other:_____	

People	Current State	Alliance Scope
		10. Alliance staff will be employed by: (Check one) ☐ Partner(s) ☐ In-house ☐ In-house and Partner(s)
	11. T&D employees: (Check all that apply) ☐ Are not available ☐ May interview for positions with alliance ☐ Will be available to transfer knowledge during transition ☐ Must be hired (explain): _____ _____	
	12. Indicate the # of T&D full-time staff at corporate and site/business:	**12. Indicate the # of proposed full-time alliance staff:**

12. Indicate the # of T&D full-time staff at corporate and site/business:

	Corp.	Site
Sr. Exec.	_____	_____
Manager	_____	_____
Bus. Liaison	_____	_____
Consultant	_____	_____
Trainer	_____	_____
CSR	_____	_____
DTP	_____	_____
Financial Coord.	_____	_____
Resource Coord.	_____	_____
Admin.	_____	_____
Total	_____	_____

12. Indicate the # of proposed full-time alliance staff:

	Corp.	Site
Sr. Exec.	_____	_____
Manager	_____	_____
Bus. Liaison	_____	_____
Consultant	_____	_____
Trainer	_____	_____
CSR	_____	_____
DTP	_____	_____
Financial Coord.	_____	_____
Resource Coord.	_____	_____
Admin.	_____	_____
Total	_____	_____

Process	Current State	Alliance Scope
		13. Processes the alliance will install: ☐ Leadership and Management ☐ Relationship Management ☐ Learning Technology ☐ Knowledge Management ☐ Delivery ☐ Delivery Operations: ☐ Registration and Participant Communications ☐ Facilities Scheduling ☐ Instructor and Vendor Communications ☐ Managing Projects and Course Finances ☐ Materials Ordering ☐ Publications and Fulfillment ☐ Develop and Maintain Catalog of Offerings ☐ In-house Resource Network ☐ Resourcing ☐ Vendor Management ☐ Business Operations: ☐ Finance and Accounting/Billing System ☐ Reporting System ☐ Communications and Marketing ☐ Human Resources ☐ Information Systems Support ☐ Office Administration

Process	Current State	Alliance Scope
	14. Registration handled via: (Check all that apply) ☐ Intra-company mail ☐ Email ☐ Intranet ☐ Internet ☐ Interactive voice response system ☐ Phone—without consultation ☐ Phone—with consultation ☐ Other:_____	**14. Registration will be handled via:** (Check all that apply) ☐ Intra-company mail ☐ Email ☐ Intranet ☐ Internet ☐ Interactive voice response system ☐ Phone—without consultation ☐ Phone—with consultation ☐ Other:_____
	15. List current registration software: – – –	**15. Alliance registration software:** – – –
	16. T&D facilities are: (Check all that apply) ☐ Dedicated on-site ☐ Non-dedicated on-site ☐ External facilities ☐ Other:_____	**16. Alliance T&D facilities will be:** (Check all that apply) ☐ Dedicated on-site ☐ Non-dedicated on-site ☐ External facilities ☐ Other:_____

Process	Current State	Alliance Scope
	17. Are there adequate on-site facilities for training? ☐ Yes ☐ No	**17. Will there be adequate on-site facilities for training?** ☐ Yes ☐ No
	18. How are facilities scheduled?	**18. How will facilities be scheduled?**
	19. Currently charge back? Based on? ☐ Allocation (explain) ☐ Use (explain)	**19. Billing will be:** (Check all that apply) ☐ Based on contract ☐ Priced on PCWS ☐ Authorized by customer in advance ☐ Sent directly to each business unit ☐ Other:_____
	20. Desktop publishing is done by: ☐ On-site DTP ☐ Alternative contract resources ☐ Partner(s) ☐ Other:_____	**20. Desktop publishing will be done by:** ☐ On-site DTP ☐ Alternative contract resources ☐ Partner(s) ☐ Other:_____

Infrastructure	Current State	Alliance Scope
	21. DTP software used for: Word processing: _____ _____ Presentations:_____ _____	**21. DTP software will be:** – Microsoft Word – Microsoft PowerPoint
	22. Printing and fulfillment is handled by: Printer:_____ _____ Fulfillment:_____ _____	**22. Printing and fulfillment will be handled by:** ☐ Partner(s) ☐ Alternative contracted suppliers ☐ On-site print shop
	23. Primary source of instructors/facilitators is: ☐ T&D staff ☐ Non-T&D staff ☐ Former employees ☐ Vendors	**23. Primary source of instructors/facilitators will be:** ☐ T&D staff ☐ Non-T&D staff ☐ Former employees ☐ Partner(s)
	24. Vendor contracts are currently managed by: ☐ T&D organization ☐ Purchasing Dept. ☐ No contracts	**24. Vendor contracts will be managed by:** ☐ Partner(s) ☐ In-house ☐ Other:_____

Infrastructure	Current State	Alliance Scope
	25. The in-house operating system is: ☐ DOS ☐ Windows 3.1 ☐ Windows 95 ☐ Macintosh ☐ Other:_____	
	26. The HRIS system is: ☐ PeopleSoft ☐ SAP ☐ Other:_____ _____	
	27. What is the % of employee population with: – PCs on their desks _____ – Email on their desks _____	
	28. The email system is:	

Customer	Current State	Alliance Scope
	29. What % of T&D dollars are spent by each region? – North America _____ – Latin America _____ – Europe _____ – Asia/Pacific _____	**29. Which regions will be served by the alliance?** (Identify primary locations) ☐ North America: _____ _____ ☐ Latin America: _____ _____ _____ ☐ Europe: _____ _____ _____ ☐ Asia/Pacific: _____ _____ _____
	30. What % of T&D dollars are spent by each business/function? – _____ ___% – _____ ___% – _____ ___% – _____ ___% – _____ ___% – _____ ___% – _____ ___%	**30. Which business/functions will be served by the alliance?** ☐ _____ ☐ _____ ☐ _____ ☐ _____ ☐ _____ ☐ _____ ☐ _____

Customer	Current State	Alliance Scope
	31. What % of participant hours are from each of these groups? – Senior Executives ____% – Management ____% – Marketing ____% – Customer Serv. ____% – Manufacturing ____% – Administrative ____% **Total** **100%**	**31. For which participants will the alliance provide training** (Check all that apply and estimate %) ☐ Senior Executives ____% ☐ Management ____% ☐ Marketing ____% ☐ Customer Serv. ____% ☐ Manufacturing ____% ☐ Administrative ____% **Total** **100%**
	32. When is the peak demand for training? (Rank from 1–4 where 1 is top priority.) __ Jan-Feb-Mar __ Apr-May-June __ July-Aug-Sept __ Oct-Nov-Dec	
	33. What is the current level of customer satisfaction with training? (Rate from 1–5 where 5 is the highest) – Senior Exec. _____ – Managers _____ – Participants _____	
	34. What are the typical lead-time requirements from request to delivery?	

Results	Current State	Alliance Scope
	35. What are the reasons for establishing the alliance? (Rank from 1–11 [or higher] where 1 is top priority)	
	– Link training to strategies and key business issues _____	
	– Measure training impact on business and investment _____	
	– Reduce the total cost/investment _____	
	– Reduce the unit cost of training (per person per day) _____	
	– Convert fixed costs to variable (pay for use) _____	
	– Provide clear accountability for operational efficiency and impact of work _____	
	– Increase responsiveness and speed _____	
	– Provide consistent high-quality training across the corporation _____	
	– Implement distributed learning/ alternatives to classroom training _____	
	– Increase efficiency and effectiveness of T&D operations _____	
	– Access and leverage right resources for needs _____	
	– Other:_____ _____	
	– Other:_____ _____	

Results	Current State	Alliance Scope
	36. Current T&D metrics: – Total T&D expenditures _____ – Unit cost per participant per day (includes instructor materials, room, **F&B****) _____ – Training expenditures as % of payroll _____ – Training expenditures per employee _____ – Average # of training days per employee _____ – Ratio of training staff to employees _____	
	37. T&D reporting includes: (Check all that apply) ☐ # participant hours ☐ Costs ☐ Instructor ratings ☐ Course ratings ☐ Participant learning ☐ Application of learning ☐ Impact on business results ☐ Other:_____	**37. Alliance reports will include:** (Check all that apply) ☐ # participant hours ☐ Costs ☐ Instructor ratings ☐ Course ratings ☐ Participant learning ☐ Application of learning ☐ Impact on business results ☐ Other:_____
	38. Frequency of T&D organization reporting is: (Check all that apply) ☐ Monthly ☐ Quarterly ☐ Annually	**38. Frequency of alliance reporting will be:** (Check all that apply) ☐ Monthly ☐ Quarterly ☐ Annually

Results	Current State	Alliance Scope
	39. Audience for T&D organization report is: – _____ – _____ – _____ – _____	**39. Audience for alliance reporting will be:** ☐ Alliance Advisory Board ☐ Alliance Staff ☐ Business Unit Leaders ☐ Other:_____
Ongoing training during transition		**40. How will ongoing needs be addressed during the transition?** ☐ Moratorium on training ☐ Curent T&D staff ☐ Transition team
Project Timeline		**41. What are customer expectation re: timeline?** (List date as mm/dd/yy. Note: Number in parens is minimum number of business days from launch.) – Transition contract signed ____ – Alliance contract signed ____ – Transition team on board ____ – In-house employees selected ____ – Staffing complete (90) ____ – Infrastructure installed (90) ____ – Courses announced (90) ____ – Relationship managers making customer calls (105) ____ – Participants in training (120) ____

Alliance Delivery Macro Process Map

Planning your work, and most especially establishing clear account-abilities, is essential to meeting customer expectations and to achieving operating efficiency. These three frames are abstracted from a much longer Moore Learning Alliance chart of project work flows that specifies accountabilities and timing from the proposal and contract all the way through measuring and capturing learnings.

Alliance Delivery Macro Process Map

➤ TIME ➤	PROJECT PHASE 5: Deliver ➤ TIME ➤
Function/Role	Sequence of Activities
Relationship Manager (RM)	
Director, Capability Development (DCD)	
Customer Service Representative (CSR)	Runs the class (CSR-30)
Resource Coordinator (RC)	
Desktop Publisher/ Production/Coordinator and Fulfillment (DTP)	Fulfillment facility provides course material (DTP-6)
Course Facilitator/Instructor (CF)	Facilitates the class (CF-1) → Leaves room in the condition he/she found it (CF-2) ➤
Financial Coordinator (FC)	
Administrator (ADM)	

Alliance Delivery Macro Process Map

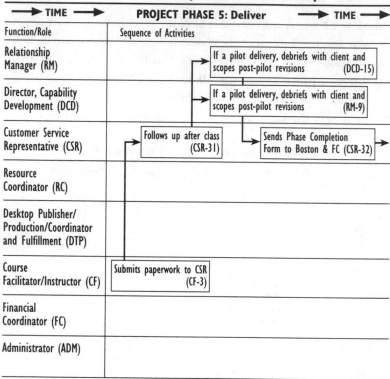

TIME →	PROJECT PHASE 5: Deliver → TIME →
Function/Role	Sequence of Activities
Relationship Manager (RM)	If a pilot delivery, debriefs with client and scopes post-pilot revisions (DCD-15)
Director, Capability Development (DCD)	If a pilot delivery, debriefs with client and scopes post-pilot revisions (RM-9)
Customer Service Representative (CSR)	Follows up after class (CSR-31) Sends Phase Completion Form to Boston & FC (CSR-32)
Resource Coordinator (RC)	
Desktop Publisher/ Production/Coordinator and Fulfillment (DTP)	
Course Facilitator/Instructor (CF)	Submits paperwork to CSR (CF-3)
Financial Coordinator (FC)	
Administrator (ADM)	

Alliance Delivery Macro Process Map

→ TIME →	PROJECT PHASE 6: Measure → TIME →
Function/Role	Sequence of Activities

Relationship Manager (RM)
- Discusses results with client (RM-10)
- Monitors ongoing delivery issues with Client-Focused Team (RM-11)

Director, Capability Development (DCD)
- Provides measurement data and reports results to stakeholders (DCD-16)

Customer Service Representative (CSR)
- Enters PSQ (LI) and Instructor Feedback Form into measurement process (CSR-33)
- Receives Measurement Report from Boston Operations (CSR-34)
- Verifies/approves Training Provider (vendor) invoices (CSR-35)

Resource Coordinator (RC)
- Codes and approves ResNet payments (RC-5)

Desktop Publisher/ Production/Coordinator and Fulfillment (DTP)

Course Facilitator/Instructor (CF)

Financial Coordinator (FC)

Administrator (ADM)

Notes

Preface
1. Includes companies with 100 or more employees. "Training Magazine's Industry Report," *Training Magazine,* 1997.

Chapter 1
1. Justin Martin, "Lifelong Learning Spells Earnings," *Fortune,* July 6, 1998.
2. Patricia A. Galagan, "Go With the Cash Flow," *Training & Development,* November 1997.
3. David Stamp, "Wall Street Comes Wooing," *Training Magazine,* November 1997.
4. John E. Hunter, et. al., "Individual Differences in Output Variability as a Function of Job Complexity," *Journal of Applied Psychology* vol. 75, 1995.
5. Cited with permission of General Electric Corporation.
6. "Training for Business Success," *The 1997 Oxford Training Review,* Oxford Training, Oxfordshire, UK.
7. Thomas A. Stewart, "Is This Job Really Necessary?" *Fortune,* January 12, 1998.

Chapter 2
1. Laurie J. Bassi and Daniel P. McMurrer, "The 1998 ASTD State of the Industry Report," *Training & Development,* January 1998.
2. Laurie J. Bassi and Daniel P. McMurrer, "Training Investment Can Mean Financial Performance," *Training & Development,* May 1998.
3. Theresa M. Welbourne and Alice O. Andrews, "Predicting the Performance of Initial Public Offerings: Should Human Resource Management Be in the Equation?" *Academy of Management Journal* vol. 39, no. 4, 1996.

4. Bassi and McMurrer, "The 1998 ASTD State of the Industry Report."

5. Donald Kirkpatrick, *Evaluating Training Programs: The Four Levels* (San Francisco: Berrett-Koehler, 1994).

6. Anthony P. Carnevale and Eric R. Shultz, "Evaluation Framework, Design, and Reports," *Training & Development,* July 1990.

7. Brian Hackett, "The Value of Training in the Era of Intellectual Capital, a Research Report," The Conference Board, 1997.

Chapter 3

1. Richard Whitely and Diane Hessan, *Customer Centered Growth: Five Proven Strategies for Building Competitive Advantage* (Reading, Massachusetts: Addison-Wesley, 1996).

Chapter 6

1. Noel M. Tichy and Stratford Sherman, *Control Your Destiny Or Someone Else Will* (New York: HarperBusiness, 1994).

2. Cited with permission of The Outsourcing Institute.

3. The Yankee Group, October 1995.

4. Sally Platt, "Let's Take this Outside," *Training Magazine,* June 1997.

5. Marc Hequet, "Can You Outsource Your Brain?" *Training Magazine,* December 1994.

6. Ibid.

7. Paul A. Strassmann, "Outsourcing, Miracle Cure or Emetic?" *Across the Board,* May 1998.

8. Cited with permission of NCR Corporation.

Index

About the Authors

David van Adelsberg is Chief Executive of Forum Europe Limited and Executive Vice President of The Forum Corporation. He oversees all of Forum's operations in Europe and is responsible for multinational accounts. Edward A. Trolley is a Senior Vice President of The Forum Corporation responsible for development and leadership of Forum's Training Management business.

In 1993, van Adelsberg and Trolley led the team that helped form The Learning Alliance at DuPont, a landmark agreement resulting in Forum's management of DuPont's global training and development worldwide.

Ed Trolley was then Manager of Training and Education for DuPont, a 110,000-person multinational corporation. Over the preceding 23 years, he had held line leadership positions in three different DuPont strategic business units and two functional units. David van Adelsberg had joined Forum in 1992 after holding a variety of sales, marketing, and management positions in both an entrepreneurial start-up and IBM, where he helped pioneer IBM's entry into "outsourcing" of information systems management. Trolley and van Adelsberg blended their experience and perspective to conceive and then implement the strategic insourcing concept described in *Running Training Like a Business.*

Subsequently, van Adelsberg directed the growth and expansion of Forum's Training Management business, leading Forum initiatives at several companies to transform training from a function-oriented activity to an internal business that delivers tangible return on investment. A graduate of Drexel University with a B.S. in Business, van Adelsberg currently resides in London, England, with his wife, Lisa, and their son, Hunter.

Trolley joined Forum in 1996 and has since been engaged by many firms to help them increase training's effectiveness and efficiency by

Running Training Like a Business. A graduate of Case Institute of Technology with a B.S. in Management Sciences, Trolley lives in Wilmington, Delaware, with his wife, Becky, and their daughter, Emily.

About the Forum Corporation

Forum is a global leader in developing innovative workplace learning solutions. Forum's offices are strategically located throughout North America, Europe, and Asia to provide international reach with the benefits of local presence. Forum has delivered measurable business results to more that 1,200 companies worldwide and continues to expand throughout the international marketplace.

The Forum Corporation
One Exchange Place
Boston, MA 02109
Tel: 617.523.7300
800.FORUM.11
Fax: 617.973.2001
Web site: www.forum.com

Forum Europe Limited
Orion House
5 Upper St. Martin's Lane
London WC2H 9EA
England
Tel: (44) 171 497 5555
Fax: (44) 171 379 9870

Berrett-Koehler Publishers

BERRETT-KOEHLER is an independent publisher of books, periodicals, and other publications at the leading edge of new thinking and innovative practice on work, business, management, leadership, stewardship, career development, human resources, entrepreneurship, and global sustainability.

Since the company's founding in 1992, we have been committed to supporting the movement toward a more enlightened world of work by publishing books, periodicals, and other publications that help us to integrate our values with our work and work lives, and to create more humane and effective organizations.

We have chosen to focus on the areas of work, business, and organizations, because these are central elements in many people's lives today. Furthermore, the work world is going through tumultuous changes, from the decline of job security to the rise of new structures for organizing people and work. We believe that change is needed at all levels—individual, organizational, community, and global—and our publications address each of these levels.

We seek to create new lenses for understanding organizations, to legitimize topics that people care deeply about but that current business orthodoxy censors or considers secondary to bottom-line concerns, and to uncover new meaning, means, and ends for our work and work lives.

See next page for other books from Berrett-Koehler Publishers

Selected Titles from
Berrett-Koehler Publishers